# Early Freud and Late Freud

We are living in a period when Freud's *œuvre* is under constant attack and is read less and less. For many years, Ilse Grubrich-Simitis, well known as an editor of Freud's manuscripts, has advocated a new reading of Freud's texts, in order that their exact detail and innovative power be fully revealed. *Early Freud and Late Freud* combines two examples of such a reading. The first essay is devoted to the earliest psychoanalytic book, *Studies on Hysteria*, which was written with Josef Breuer. The second essay is a study of Freud's last book, *Moses and Monotheism*.

The essay on *Studies on Hysteria* demonstrates why that work is indeed the 'primal book' of psychoanalysis, and how its emphasis on trauma in the genesis of psychic illness became a basic element of modern psychoanalytic thinking.

In *Moses and Monotheism*, Freud returns to his early trauma theory of the aetiology of neurosis, which he had disregarded for many years in favour of drive theory and the accentuation of phantasies. Freud was by now faced with the traumatic threat of Nazi persecution, and appears to have responded by intensifying his self-analysis, as if seeking contact with his early self. The author applies the psychoanalytic method to the Moses manuscripts and postulates that it was the dramatic self-curative process that facilitated Freud's late insights into archaic forms of defence, such as 'splitting'. These insights in turn indicated the path that modern psychoanalysis was to follow, and are understood in this book in a way that leads to the emergence of a substantially modified picture of early Freud and late Freud.

**Ilse Grubrich-Simitis** is a psychoanalyst in private practice in Frankfurt. She is a member of the International Psychoanalytical Association and a training and supervising analyst of the German Psychoanalytical Association.

# THE NEW LIBRARY OF PSYCHOANALYSIS

The New Library of Psychoanalysis was launched in 1987 in association with the Institute of Psycho-Analysis, London. Its purpose is to facilitate a greater and more widespread appreciation of what psychoanalysis is really about and to provide a forum for increasing mutual understanding between psychoanalysts and those working in other disciplines such as history, linguistics, literature, medicine, philosophy, psychology and the social sciences. It is intended that the titles selected for publication in the series should deepen and develop psychoanalytic thinking and technique, contribute to psychoanalysis from outside, or contribute to other disciplines from a psychoanalytical perspective.

The Institute, together with the British Psycho-Analytic Society, runs a low-fee psychoanalytic clinic, organizes lectures and scientific events concerned with psychoanalysis, publishes the *International Journal of Psycho-Analysis* (which now incorporates the *International Review of Psycho-Analysis*), and runs the only training course in the UK in psychoanalysis leading to membership of the International Psychoanalytical Association – the body which preserves internationally agreed standards of training, of professional entry and of professional ethics and practice for psychoanalysis as initiated and developed by Sigmund Freud. Distinguished members of the Institute have included Michael Balint, Wilfred Bion, Ronald Fairbairn, Anna Freud, Ernest Jones, Melanie Klein, John Rickman and Donald Winnicott.

Volumes 1–11 in the series have been prepared under the general editorship of David Tuckett, with Ronald Britton and Eglé Laufer as associate editors. Subsequent volumes are under the general editorship of Elizabeth Bott Spillius, with, from Volume 17, Donald Campbell, Michael Parsons, Rosine Jozef Perelberg and David Taylor as associate editors.

# ALSO IN THIS SERIES

The publication of this title has been subsidized by Inter Nationes, Bonn, and the Köhler-Stiftung, Darmstadt.

# NEW LIBRARY OF PSYCHOANALYSIS
## 29

General editor: Elizabeth Bott Spillius

# Early Freud and Late Freud

## READING ANEW *STUDIES ON HYSTERIA* AND *MOSES AND MONOTHEISM*

### ILSE GRUBRICH-SIMITIS

Translated by Philip Slotkin

London and New York

First published in Britain in 1997
by Routledge
11 New Fetter Lane, London EC4P 4EE

Simultaneously published in the USA and Canada
by Routledge
29 West 35th Street, New York, NY 10001

Typeset in Bembo by LaserScript, Mitcham, Surrey
Printed and bound in Great Britain by
TJ International Ltd, Padstow, Cornwall

*British Library Cataloguing in Publication Data*
A catalogue record for this book is available from the British Library

*Library of Congress Cataloging in Publication Data*

Grubrich-Simitis, Ilse.
Early Freud and Late Freud: reading anew *Studies on Hysteria* and *Moses and Monotheism*/Ilse Grubrich-Simitis; translated by Philip Slotkin.
p. cm. – (New library of psychoanalysis; 29)

Includes bibliographical references and index.
1. Breuer, Josef, 1842–1925. Studien über Hysterie. 2. Freud, Sigmund,
1856–1939. Der Mann Moses und die monotheistische Religion. 3. Hysteria.
4. Moses (Biblical leader). 5. Egyptian literature–Relation to the Old Testament.
6. Monotheism. 7. Psychology, Religious. I. Title. II. Series.
RC532.B73G78 1997 97-12958

616.89' 17–dc21 CIP

ISBN 0–415–14843–X
ISBN 0–415–14844–8 (pbk)

# Contents

# List of figures

Thanks are due to Frau Dr Irblich, Österreichische Nationalbibliothek, Handschriften- und Inkunabel-Sammlung, Vienna, for the reproductions of Figures 2 and 3. Sigmund Freud Copyrights, Colchester, and S. Fischer Verlag, Frankfurt, kindly gave permission for Figures 4–8 to be reproduced here.

# Preliminary Note

This publication was not originally conceived as a book. The two essays of which it consists were composed at different times.

I wrote the first piece, 'The Primal Book of Psychoanalysis', representing *early Freud*, for the centenary of the appearance of Breuer's and Freud's *Studies on Hysteria*. S. Fischer, the publishers of Freud's works in Germany, brought out a reprint of the first edition to mark this anniversary in 1995 and my essay was intended as an accompanying commentary. An expanded version, on which the present translation is based, was printed in the December 1995 issue of the journal *Psyche*. A few notes on precursors of Breuer's and Freud's research were also finally added.

The essay on *late Freud* was in fact written previously. My research on Freud's manuscripts included work on those of *Moses and Monotheism*. I put forward my gradually emerging hypotheses for the first time in the Sigmund Freud Lecture in Frankfurt in 1989. The revised and expanded version of 'Freud's Study of Moses as a Daydream', from which the English translation was made, was published by Fischer Taschenbuch Verlag in 1994. The preface and parts of the preliminary note to this edition are, however, here incorporated in the introduction. A few minor additions to the five sections of the essay have also been made.

It was Elizabeth Bott Spillius, the General Editor of the New Library of Psychoanalysis, who thought of combining the two contributions in a single book with the title *Early Freud and Late Freud*, a formulation that is also hers. I am very grateful to her for this inspiring idea – for when I began to reflect on her suggestion, I realized to my surprise that there are actually more links between these two works than I had hitherto been aware of, as the following introduction is intended to show.

I wish to thank Philip Slotkin for deploying all his translation skills to confer upon my essays, as with previous writings of mine, an English form as precise as it is aesthetic.

Edwina Welham of Routledge worked hard on a number of fronts to help make the present edition a reality. Inter Nationes (Bonn) and the Köhler-Stiftung (Darmstadt) made generous contributions to the funding of the translation.

Thanks are due to Ingeborg Meyer-Palmedo, my collaborator of many years' standing on the German-language editions of Freud, for assistance and suggestions during my work on the original versions. I wish also to acknowledge the aid received at that time from Gerhard Fichtner, Eva Laible and Marion Palmedo. I am indebted to Michael Stolleis for bringing Rudolf Smend's recent lecture on Moses to my attention. Bärbel Gäthje helped find the English text of the quotations from Freud.

Mark Paterson (Sigmund Freud Copyrights) and Judith Dupont kindly allowed me to quote from some unpublished documents of Freud and Ferenczi in their respective care.

May 1996

# Introduction

The last few years have seen increasingly virulent attacks on psychoanalysis, mainly in the United States, but also in certain European countries. The principal target of these onslaughts is the figure of Sigmund Freud. 'Freud-bashing' has become an established concept and anti-Freudianism a movement. Anyone who joins it and barefacedly takes the floor has an opportunity, thanks to the media's astounding abrogation of their critical faculties in this polemical field, to spread his views abroad and make a name for himself in soapbox fashion – that is, without the need for any substantive input of his own.

The charges range from a crude and sometimes almost violent questioning of Freud's personal and professional integrity to attempts at epistemological dismantling of the claims of psychoanalysis to validity. Disregarding the nature of the phenomena with which psychoanalytic work is concerned – predominantly unconscious meanings, wishes, phantasies and affects, as well as complex processes of psychic assimilation of traumatic experiences – that is, subjectivity and intersubjectivity in the widest sense, those responsible apply causal scientific criteria of a kind now deemed obsolete even in relation to the phenomena studied by the hard natural sciences. Again, however strangely cobbled together the speculation, however blatantly tendentious the montage of quotations, casting Freud in the role of a hopeless addict or a murderer in disguise, as an adulterer, plagiarist or careerist, contemptuous of his patients and out to oppress his pupils, and so on, everything is accepted with credulity. At any rate, whatever the simplification, abstruse spurious logic and downright falsification, it is clear that none of those concerned need fear for their reputations as serious academics or credible investigative journalists.

This state of affairs calls for explanation. On the one hand, there seems to be a widespread and uncontrollably powerful need to get rid once and for all of the disagreeable and uncanny insights about ourselves which Freud and psychoanalysis have imposed on us. On the other hand, the ubiquity and stubborn persistence of the attacks must surely be regarded as a sign of the still unbroken vitality of Freudian thought. After all, the ageing and obsolescence of scientific ideas are otherwise a silent process that is barely perceptible to the public at large. Such ideas are simply deemed no longer worth mentioning and there is no further need for noisy opposition to them. So if the present commotion were a token of the unexhausted potential of psychoanalysis to fathom the depths and thereby facilitate understanding of central aspects of the human condition, the Freud-bashers' compulsive seeking of the limelight might perhaps be an unconscious manifestation of the cannibal's ancient hope of partaking in the potency of the mighty enemy by destroying and then incorporating him.

There has been no lack of attacks on psychoanalysis since the earliest days of its existence. As Freud, already well advanced in years, wrote to Albert Einstein on 26 March 1929:

> All our attention is directed to the outside, whence dangers threaten and satisfactions beckon. From the inside, we want only to be left in peace. So if someone tries to turn our awareness inward, [...] then our whole organization resists – just as, for example, the oesophagus and the urethra resist any attempt to reverse their normal direction of passage. The world is then united in contradiction [...]. And everyone finds contradiction so easy precisely in the field of psychology. Without specialized preparation, no one can permit himself a judgement in astronomy, physics or chemistry. Unless one is simply crazy [...], one will beware of contradicting science if one has not fulfilled this condition. This does not hold for psychology. Every man is a connoisseur of the mind, every man knows just as well, or better, without having gone to any trouble.[1]

Although Freud here uses the general term 'psychology', there is no doubt that he means his psychology of the unconscious – for it alone, even in those days, caused critics, driven by their affects and lacking competence and qualifications, to presume to make judgements. It alone triggers the reflex of bristling repudiation that Freud attempts to characterize by the metaphor of reversal of the normal direction of passage of the oesophagus and urethra.

His diagnosis that the 'unnatural' practice of turning the attention inward is bound to provoke resistances retains all its validity today. Indeed, the resistances may well have become stronger since Freud's time, because the satisfactions that beckon and the dangers that threaten from outside –

---

1 Quoted in Grubrich-Simitis 1995: 117.

that is, the stimuli which, according to his description, bind our attention *externally* – have now been joined by new ones. For some years there have been unmistakable signals that – not only according to the calendar but also culturally – we stand upon the threshold of a new age. Interactive media communication, navigation in cyberspace, the shift from words to images, the hostility towards differentiation and distinction, the idolization of brevity, the short term and acceleration, and so forth – all these make the turning inward of attention that characterizes the Freudian method more and more improbable and completely unnatural in a longer-range perspective. Moreover, few welcome the material brought to the surface by long-term, high-frequency psychoanalytic work – on the one hand, the archaic unconscious internal world of man in its unfathomable complexity, which defies rational control and programmability and incessantly generates meanings, and, on the other, the undeniable dependence of the early development of psychic structure and of the ability to think on reliable emotional object relations. That is because this material exposes as an illusion the idea that not only professional routines but also human life and experience themselves can be simplified and facilitated to an ever increasing extent. The protest against this postmodern ideal, a protest registered by psychoanalytic work if only because of the direction and results of its research, may be one of the reasons why anti-Freudianism, whose aim is the total stripping of credibility from psychoanalysis and its founder, seems to satisfy a collective need today.

So although the external binding of attention described by Freud in his letter to Einstein has since intensified further, truck with the electronic information technologies now developing at breakneck pace seems at the same time to make for an increasing loss of reality in people's everyday lives. Might insistence on the link with one's private unconscious *internal* reality – a connection that can be maintained only by the expenditure of much effort – prove to be an effective antidote to losing oneself in the new *virtual* reality, to the progressive enfeeblement of one's capacity for responsible intercourse with the threatening and threatened *external* reality? If so, advocacy of the continued handing down and further development of the psychoanalytic method, the only one so far existing whereby this connection with the unconscious internal world can be made, would not merely serve the preservation of a valuable cultural heritage: rather than a luxury, or even merely a therapeutic desideratum for the relief of human suffering, it would be an elementary social necessity.

★

One reason why the anti–Freudians are so readily believed is surely that Freud's texts are becoming increasingly unknown. The Freud-bashers know, and bank on the fact, that, given the flood of stimuli from omnipresent information technology, withdrawal into 'the archaic silence of the book'[2] is now tantamount to an act of resistance. For given a careful reading of the texts of the founder of psychoanalysis, no one could possibly, even for a moment, take seriously, say, the assertion that after correcting his initial seduction theory he completely disregarded traumatic factors in his conception of the genesis of neurosis and concentrated exclusively on the aetiological role of unconscious phantasies or drive-related aspects. The inaccuracy of this proposition is obvious to, and easily demonstrated by, anyone familiar with the relevant writings of Freud. It is based either on ignorance of the *œuvre* or on deliberate falsification, if not on a conscious desire to mislead the reader and the public.[3]

In this situation, a return to Freud's texts – however out of keeping this may be with the times – may be commended. It will enable one firstly to form an opinion of one's own on the Freud-bashers' arguments and secondly to gain an impression of what would be lost if the Freudian heritage, and in particular the application of the psychoanalytic method, were to cease to be handed down in the foreseeable future. Moreover, what is advocated here is a radical reading anew of his writings, with a view to rediscovering them or indeed to discovering them for the first time – for, like all great texts, they are inexhaustible. For this purpose, a particular reading attitude is recommended, made up of unobtrusiveness, careful alertness and respect even for the most seemingly insignificant detail – an oscillation between proximity and distance that will assure the texts of sufficient free space to reveal themselves in all their independence. To put this in negative terms, in order to have any chance of perceiving what Freud was trying to express in his writings at the time of their composition while in the midst of the process of understanding, the reader must approach them *not* from a meta-level, *not* as it were looking down from above, and *not* from a vantage point of 'superior' knowledge – that is, *not* solely from the plane of present-day psychoanalytic theory and practice. The risk otherwise is of encountering nothing but his own conscious or unconscious expectations or, alternatively, the babel of later interpreters' voices drowning out everything else.

Of course, a 'naïve' reading of this kind, directed towards maximum authenticity of understanding, is but approximately feasible. We are, after

---

2   Benjamin 1980 [1928]: 103.
3   Cf., for example, Grubrich-Simitis 1988 [1987].

all, not contemporaries of Freud, and can at most keep in the background, but not totally suspend, knowledge we have since acquired. The attitude commended to the reader can perhaps best be likened to that of 'evenly suspended attention', which we assume in relation to the analysand's communications in the course of our analytic work.

★

I have done my best to adopt this special reading attitude in my work on the two essays brought together in this volume. In the case of the Moses contribution, composed earlier, with its new reading of *Moses and Monotheism*,[4] this approach came about by itself, so to speak intuitively. I had embarked in the 1980s on the study of the Freud manuscripts kept in the Manuscript Division of the Library of Congress. When, during the course of this research, I was invited to give the Sigmund Freud Lecture in Frankfurt in the year of the fiftieth anniversary of the death of the founder of psychoanalysis, I chose a subject associated with the work on which I was then engaged: I proposed to examine in detail some peculiarities that had caught my attention, and raised questions in my mind, in the bundle of the Moses manuscripts; these peculiarities are described in more detail below, at the beginning of the essay and in its appendix. When I began reading Freud's last book anew, I had no ready-made hypothesis or theory for which I might have wanted to seek evidence. I read so to speak without preconceived notions, albeit in the hope that, if only I could remain sufficiently alert towards the text, I might learn something that would help me to discover a meaning in those peculiarities of the surviving manuscripts.

This special attitude, whose aim is authentic understanding, was reflected in the writing of my book *Back to Freud's Texts*, which appeared – in its original German edition – after the essay on Moses[5] and summarizes the results of my study of the manuscripts. Later, when I reread Breuer's and Freud's *Studies on Hysteria*[6] for the centenary of the publication of this 'primal book' of psychoanalysis with a view to writing about my impressions – as an invitation to the reader to embark on a similar adventure himself – I consciously set out from the beginning to adopt this attitude of not obtruding on the text so as to allow it the free space it needs.

---

4  Freud 1939a.
5  Grubrich-Simitis 1996 [1993].
6  Breuer and Freud 1895.

However, this attitude is not the only link between the two essays. There are a number of other points of contact. Before discussing these, I should like to make a few specific comments on each of the texts.

★

In Freud's letter to Albert Einstein quoted above, the diagnosis that the turning inward of attention always gives rise to resistance relates directly to the psychoanalytic method itself, the revolutionary invention of which afforded systematic access to the human internal world for the first time. From this point of view, the application of this method appears to be an enterprise that *goes against the grain*. So if it is true that from 'the inside, we want only to be left in peace', this revolutionary production is threatened again and again with renewed repression. Psychoanalysts do not necessarily realize this, because for them the method is taken for granted as if it had existed always. To remind oneself of the innovative improbability of its creation, it seems appropriate to place oneself back as concretely as possible in the context in which it came into being. It may be noted in passing that it is surely no accident that the majority of Freud-bashers are non-clinicians. Nowhere are we more directly confronted with the force and ubiquity of unconscious processes – but also with the efficacy of the psychoanalytic method – than in the daily course of clinical work. Compact analytic experience of one's own thus helps one endure the exacting demands imposed by Freudian thought.

The centenary of the publication of *Studies on Hysteria* provided a welcome opportunity, in reading Breuer's and Freud's joint work, of literally sharing in their experience of the discovery of specific analytic listening. My purpose in writing the first of these two essays was in fact not to impart something new but to bring vigorously to life something old that is in danger of being forgotten. By carefully reading anew the primal book of psychoanalysis, the reader will find it easier to imagine the radical nature of the innovation then introduced by Breuer and Freud to the medical culture of their age.

This innovation was radical even though much that we now consider to be genuinely psychoanalytic appears in this text at most in embryo. For example, we can observe isolated instances when the two physicians showed empathy with their patients, but then sometimes abruptly withdrew it again. We must in such a case remind ourselves that in those days the concept and phenomenon of empathy were not yet even in sight, and that, when Breuer and Freud momentarily empathized, it was so to speak by virtue of the prevailing bourgeois emotional culture. Our reading will also make it clear to us that, when Freud introduces the concept of 'transference' in the very last pages of the book, he is still using it in the narrow sense of a 'false connection' between the past and the recent.

Ultimately, even the discovery of specifically analytic listening was in fact confined at first to the concrete incorporation of the ear as a sense organ in the process of examination and treatment and to the manifest surface of the incoming text: what information did this text provide on the sought-for logical connection between a real event or experience and the form assumed by the symptom? In *The Question of Lay Analysis*, late Freud was to emphasize once again this elementary process of acoustic–auditory exchange in the following laconic statement: 'The analyst agrees upon a fixed regular hour with the patient, gets him to talk, listens to him, talks to him in his turn and gets him to listen.'[7]

Quite soon after the publication of *Studies on Hysteria*, Freud ceased to be concerned solely with the *fact* of listening and turned his attention to *how* one should listen. The further development of the concept of analytic listening – which is synonymous with the increasing differentiation of the psychoanalytic method – in the later Freud and in the subsequent generations of psychoanalysts is surely a different matter. We have learned to listen not only to the verbal communications of our analysands but also to the pitch, rhythm, volume and vibration of the voice, to the types and meanings of silence, and to the ways in which patients for their part listen to us, avert their ears from us and misunderstand us. The investigation and training of analytic listening soon came to extend beyond the mere auditory function to the more generalized level of the sensitivity and keenness of receptivity of the entire perceptual apparatus – of the diacritic system that uses the sensory organs as well as of the regressive coenaesthetic system.

Alert to the potential significance of even the tiniest details which our 'natural' perception otherwise overlooks, fails to hear or excludes, we observe verbal and preverbal or averbal manifestations, elements of dreams and phantasies, feelings and thoughts, somatic sensations such as pain, vertigo, fatigue, vigilance and the like, as well as behaviour and action, in both the analysand and ourselves. More and more new kinds of phenomena have been successively incorporated in the analytic process of understanding: transference, countertransference, acting out. Looking back, it actually seems as if, over the decades, the label 'resistance' was sometimes involuntarily applied in a pejorative sense when, in the study of

---

7  Freud 1926e: 187.

the processes taking place in the analysand and/or analyst, it was necessary for the time being to exclude from the field of view complexity that, at least at the time, could not yet have been coped with. After all, these three fields – especially countertransference and acting out – were initially seen as forms of resistance, as something that obstructed the progress of the process of understanding, before we learned to recognize and use them as rich sources of unconscious information and communication.

Hence it was, and still is, a matter of the investigation and handling of a multidimensional – conscious, preconscious and unconscious – system of resonances and transformations, of which mutually complementary models were developed in the course of time, mostly using the analogy of the earliest forms of exchange between mother and child. Examples include Winnicott's holding function or Bion's container/contained relationship and alpha function. The common ground between the various psycho-analytic schools is discernible in the uncompromising application and further development of the method. Moreover, the method is surely also the part of the Freudian heritage which, unlike some areas of theory, has lost none of its relevance today.

At any rate, what has crystallized out of the hundred-year evolution of the psychoanalytic method is by far the most subtle and powerful instrument ever for investigation of the unconscious internal world of man, and in general of human subjectivity and self-interpretation – one that is difficult to learn, difficult to hand on, and as much in need of protection as it is worth protecting. The first textual precipitate of this revolutionary production in the field of the human sciences was *Studies on Hysteria*. My essay on the 'primal book of psychoanalysis' was intended as a reminder of these facts.


Let us now turn to the essay on Moses. As already stated, certain peculiarities I had noticed in the Moses manuscripts led me to read *Moses and Monotheism* anew. However, it was only during the course of this reading that I realized fully quite *how* atypical this work is. It is distinguished from other writings of Freud, including the late ones, by an oddly flawed structure. My efforts to understand this conformation, as well as those conspicuous peculiarities of the surviving manuscripts, unexpectedly turned out to demand an attempt at psychoanalytic interpretation – that is to say, the application of the psychoanalytic method to one of Freud's works. I found to my surprise that, notwithstanding the flood of biographical literature on the founder of psychoanalysis, the old Freud was almost as unknown as the very early, infant Freud, and that *Moses and Monotheism* can serve as a refracting prism which spreads out the incoming beam into a darkly glowing spectrum that illuminates and connects the beginning and end of Freud's inner life. From this point of view, my essay on Moses can be read by itself as a variation on the theme of *Early Freud and Late Freud.*

My original intention was merely to compare the manuscript and the printed version and to reflect on the discrepancies between them. The – as it were – incidental results of this textual analysis emerged only from the reactions to my Sigmund Freud Lecture. Members of the audience told me that it had been essentially a *biographical* contribution, containing not only elements of the psychology of old age but also a sketch for an image of Freud different in some respects from the conventional one: what was impressive about the old man, apart from the reflexive force with which he overcame a final crisis of his own and metabolized it in theory, was in particular the extent to which he was torn asunder by internal tensions; it was becoming clearer how far his self-analysis had actually remained one of the principal sources of his work throughout his life. These reactions encouraged me to amplify the lecture.

Shortly after the publication of its expanded text, something rather unpredictable happened. When I originally began work on the Moses manuscripts, that wondrous last book of Freud's seemed in fact to have been substantially forgotten. What then occurred was summed up by Peter Gay in his 1993 review of my essay on Moses, by his observation that the theme of Moses had shortly afterwards suddenly become 'fashionable'.[8] In addition to various articles, two books had appeared in quick succession: *Freud and Moses: The Long Journey Home,* by Emanuel Rice,[9] and the learned treatise by Yosef Hayim Yerushalmi, *Freud's Moses: Judaism Terminable and Interminable.*[10] As the subtitles indicate and as critically analysed by Gay in his review, both authors were working with a different objective from my own – that of proving their prior conviction that Freud and his entire *œuvre* belonged in the framework of Jewish tradition, even if this had the inevitable consequence of calling into question the avowed distance from and critique of religion of the founder of psychoanalysis. However, the approach and results of my own study of Moses are unaffected by these later publications, so that a detailed response to the theses of Rice and Yerushalmi is not necessary here. Their interpretations of Moses also differ from my own attempt in that both authors adopt the more traditional

---

8 Gay 1993: 973.
9 Rice 1990.
10 Yerushalmi 1991.

standpoint of focusing on Freud's relationship with his father, whereas I found it more illuminating to reflect – however tentatively – on the early relationship with the mother for the purpose of understanding certain aspects of the manuscripts and printed text of *Moses and Monotheism*.

*

Immediately before his seventy-second birthday, Freud wrote the following to Ernest Jones on 3 May 1928: '"Young" and "old" now seem to me the most significant opposites that the human soul can harbour, and an understanding between the representatives of either group is impossible.'[11] Years before embarking on his late research on Moses, then, he was already beginning to think about the devastating modifications wrought by the process of ageing. What he told Jones may be true of each new young generation that takes its place in society with a range of different attitudes, while the subject himself has grown old. But it does not apply to the ageing person's own earlier life, to which he is often closer than someone in middle age, who fancies himself to be equidistant from the beginning and end of his own life.

At any rate, in this sense of intrapsychic intercourse with the representations of the successive phases of Freud's own life-cycle, good understanding and brisk communication seem to have existed between *early* Freud and *late* Freud. Even before the essay on *Studies on Hysteria* was in prospect, I had already pointed out in my contribution on Moses that one of Freud's concerns had been to look back explicitly at his *œuvre*, and in particular to return to his early reflections on the traumatic genesis of psychic illness and to weave them into the context of his current research. My subsequent essay on the 'primal book' then led, in effect automatically, to the reference to the aetiological ideas of late Freud – albeit still before the plan to unite the two essays between the covers of a single book.

In considering the links between my two essays, then, we should mention first the concept of *trauma*. Of course, *Studies on Hysteria* and *Moses and Monotheism* represent two completely different stages in the development of the psychoanalytic concept of trauma.

In the 'primal book of psychoanalysis', this concept has not yet completely shed the downy feathers of its origins in organic medicine: we can observe how the two authors – Freud more resolutely than Breuer – seek to translate the traditional somatic dimensions of meaning into the

---

11 Freud 1993e [1908–39]: 646.

psychic field. The medical assumption had been that a sudden injury caused by an external agency and accompanied by a tissue lesion subsequently affected the entire organism. Breuer and Freud attributed the onset of neurotic illness to the analogous irruption of an external event into the subject's life history, exceeding the capacity of the psychic apparatus appropriately to assimilate or abreact the inflowing quantity of stimuli and the affects thereby unleashed; the residues, in their view, had a permanent pathogenic effect on the entire personality of the traumatized subject in the form of a 'foreign body' or 'infiltrate'. Admittedly, in the *Studies* Freud is already working towards the idea that it is not the traumatic event as such that, so to speak indiscriminately, has harmful consequences, but that the capacity of the subject to assimilate it is correlated with his prior psychic – that is, defensive – conflict.

Then followed forty years of growth and elaboration of psychoanalysis based on Freud's research; this was the time of the actual discovery of unconscious internal reality, when his aetiological theories underwent unremitting further development. It is therefore not surprising that the concept of trauma encountered by the reader in *Moses and Monotheism* is much more complex. One of the ideas that Freud had abandoned was that of limitation to overwhelming *sexual* experiences, which had dominated the picture for a few years after the publication of the *Studies*. In *Moses and Monotheism*, the focus of his attention has shifted to the wide range of subtle *narcissistic* injuries – that is, ones that take effect only by summation or cumulation – which the child sustains during the pregenital phase of development in its dealings with its primary objects and which have the consequence of permanent alterations of the ego by way of identifications. The reader here encounters embryonic formulations of modern psycho-analytic object-relations theory, as well as fundamental components of an aetiological theory of narcissistic, borderline and psychotic disturbances.

Notwithstanding all these further developments, in *Moses and Monotheism* late Freud appears to be seeking a dialogue with his early counterpart, with the aim of himself looking back once again at his own beginnings as a psychoanalytic thinker, when he set about performing that unnatural movement outlined in the letter to Einstein: that of gradually detaching his attention from traumatic external events and turning it inwards. Now that his own life was overshadowed by such events, he seems to have been concerned to reassign more weight to trauma in the aetiological equation, thereby correcting the radical inward orientation of his perception.

Another evident link between the contents of my two essays is the *exemplification of the method*. The 'primal book' contribution is intended to illustrate the context in which this method came into being and the formulation of initial aspects of its therapeutic use, whereas in the Moses essay I firstly apply the psychoanalytic method to a Freudian text myself and secondly portray the aged investigator engaged in a retrospective reflection on the essentials of psychoanalysis, sometimes by analogy with the fundamentals of monotheism and with the conditions under which it arose; here we see Freud himself exemplifying the method by applying it to the biblical text.

There is yet another common thread, albeit less conspicuous. The two books that are the subject of my essays both have their origins in times of inner crisis. Freud's father was admittedly still alive when *Studies on Hysteria* appeared in 1895. It was not until a year later that the son, in consequence of his loss, sustained the profound emotional upset that demanded the systematization of self-analysis, to which we evidently also owe *The Interpretation of Dreams*.[12] The upset cannot have been a sudden one, for the death of the eighty-one-year-old father did not come completely out of the blue. It is a fact that during the composition of the *Studies* Freud was already suffering from various somatic complaints and in particular some alarming cardiac symptoms. His own self-perception during this period emerges from the Fliess letters: 'I, with my eternally flickering mood'.[13] Not the least of his troubles was the misery of nicotine withdrawal. Moreover, the increasing dissension with Josef Breuer, his paternal mentor, had risen to the pitch of painful and irreparable alienation even before the publication of their joint work. There can at any rate be no doubt that Freud was in crisis while working on the *Studies*. The book contains indications of his efforts at self-analysis – for example, a hint that the young investigator had already embarked on the study of his own dreams.

When Freud wrote *Moses and Monotheism*, he was rent by inner tensions and, as explained in detail in my essay on that work, this state is directly evident from the text itself. One of my theses is that Freud's last book arose out of a powerful new upsurge of his self-analytic efforts. After all, it is worth recalling here that, in his letter to Romain Rolland about a 'disturbance of memory on the Acropolis' written in 1936, late Freud, already immersed in his reflections on Moses, made self-analytic contact with early Freud and his relationship with his father.[14] One factor in Freud's explicit stressing of the poetic character of both works may be this autobiographical and self-analytic element that links them: as we know, in

---

12 Freud 1900a: cf. xxvi.
13 Freud 1985c [1887–1904]: 73 (published translation modified).
14 Freud 1936a.

the *Studies* he expresses his surprise that his case histories read 'like short stories', while not only did his book on Moses arise out of a dialogue with creative writers, but its first version was also subtitled 'A historical novel'.

★

At the end of the essay on the 'primal book of psychoanalysis', I touch upon the question of the survival of psychoanalysis, a theme that also resonates in the opening section of this introduction. Perhaps this question of survival concerns in particular the position of psychoanalysis in the public debate: is there any reason to fear that the destructive zeal of those Freud-bashers might ultimately after all prove effective – principally because careful, critical reading of the representative texts of psycho-analysis, on the one hand, and clinical psychoanalytic work proper, on the other, are now the preserve of the few?

Those few are the people and groups who, convinced of the unbroken capacity of the psychoanalytic method to fathom the depths of the mind, are steadfastly continuing their work and researching ever earlier phases and phenomena of the processes of psychic structuring. The degree of differentiation now attained in this establishment of the 'regular laws' of the preverbal or averbal exchanges between mother and child that permit the constitution of the subject, as well as in the determination of the extraordinary susceptibility of these exchanges to disturbance, inevitably sets limits to the communicability of such research results to the public at large. There are no interconnecting channels between the 'populist' pronouncements of the Freud-bashers on the one hand and the unspectacular detailed reports of those creatively working on the further development of psychoanalytic theory and practice on the other.

As discussed in the second essay in this book, while working on *Moses and Monotheism* Freud himself was concerned with the matter of the survival of psychoanalysis, albeit, of course, in the face of other threats. What was on his mind was whether his life-work would outlast the Nazi persecution. The aspect of Mosaic monotheism that fascinated him was how an uncomfortable doctrine that arouses opposition, having been suppressed, returns from repression and attains the culmination of its influence precisely because of this diphasic aspect. Significantly, he also describes in his last book another instance – namely, Darwin's theory of evolution – of a teaching whose impact has had a similar discontinuous rhythm. It is perhaps no accident that even this theory is now the subject of vigorous opposition in the United States, although it is based on 'harder' data than psychoanalysis. Freud, of course, compared the two doctrines in terms of the intensity of the narcissistic injury inflicted on mankind by each in its specific way.[15] In Tennessee, people are now manifestly no longer prepared to put up with this: a bill relativizing Charles Darwin's theory of the descent of man has been tabled in all seriousness in that State. Should it be passed, teachers who advocate the theory without at the same time presenting it as 'disputed' are liable to dismissal or other punishment.[16]

Be that as it may, notwithstanding the distortions of the Freud-bashers – and also despite the irrefutable obsolescence of certain concepts and theories – precisely the work of the founder of psychoanalysis has displayed a remarkable resistance to being consigned to oblivion even among the public at large; and that is surely because of its subject matter and how this subject matter is investigated and presented. It concerns the vicissitudes of human development and the fundamental conflicts that recur in each new generation because they are rooted in processes of biological maturation that cannot as yet be influenced by technology. The specific method of investigation, apart from clinical work, is essentially that of lifelong self-analysis. For that reason Freud's *œuvre* amounts to a moving, albeit mostly concealed, confession – and it moves us largely on account of the beauty of the prose in which Freud as a writer bequeathed his work to us. This beauty is not ornamental, not a mere accessory but, because it belongs to the very substance of the *œuvre*, helps Freud to make it possible for us to reconstruct the process of his observing, understanding and theorizing.

---

15 Cf., for example, Freud 1917a: 7ff.
16 Cf. a report by Leo Wieland in the *Frankfurter Allgemeine Zeitung*, 23 March 1996, no. 71: 3.

# The Primal Book of Psychoanalysis:
## *Studies on Hysteria* a hundred years on

I

The great French neuropathologist Jean-Martin Charcot died in the summer of 1893. When Sigmund Freud was not yet thirty, on his study trip to Paris, he had attended Charcot's lectures at his Salpêtrière clinic for some months in 1885 and 1886 and become acquainted with the master's novel research on hysteria. It was an encounter which, as we know, was instrumental in the transition, in Freud's intellectual development, from neuropathology to psychopathology. In his obituary[1] Freud describes how, through the authority of Charcot, hysteria had at a stroke become the focus of general attention. Charcot had restored dignity to the topic and vouched for the genuineness of the symptoms. Until then, such patients had been met with a scornful smile because they were considered to be malingerers. For the first time, what was in those days a widespread illness became an object of serious scientific concern.[2]

Freud goes on to outline the approach to solving the riddle of hysteria as follows:

A quite unbiassed [sic] observer might have arrived at this conclusion: if I find someone in a state which bears all the signs of a painful affect – weeping, screaming and raging – the conclusion seems probable that a mental process is going on in him of which those physical phenomena

---

1 Freud 1893f.
2 Hysteria had in fact been a matter of serious scientific concern before Charcot, as Alan Gauld has recently shown in his monograph *A History of Hypnotism* (1992). (I am indebted to G.W. Pigman III for drawing my attention to this work.) Cf., for example, the in many respects astonishing papers published by C.M.E.E. Azam (1876a and b, 1877) on the then famous hysteria patient Félida X, whom he had carefully observed since as far back as 1858, as well as on a case of male hysteria, Albert X (1877: 580f.).

15

are the appropriate expression. A healthy person, if he were asked, would be in a position to say what impression it was that was tormenting him; but the hysteric would answer that he did not know. The problem would at once arise of how it is that a hysterical patient is overcome by an affect about whose cause he asserts that he knows nothing. If we keep to our conclusion that a corresponding psychical process *must* be present, and if nevertheless we believe the patient when he denies it; if we bring together the many indications that the patient is behaving as though he *does* know about it; and if we enter into the history of the patient's life and find some occasion, some trauma, which would appropriately evoke precisely those expressions of feeling – then everything points to one solution: the patient is in a special state of mind in which all his impressions or his recollections of them are no longer held together by an associative chain, a state of mind in which it is possible for a recollection to express its affect by means of somatic phenomena without the group of the other mental processes, the ego, knowing about it or being able to intervene to prevent it. If we had called to mind the familiar psychological difference between sleep and waking, the strangeness of our hypothesis might have seemed less.[3]

Freud begins his next paragraph with the surprising observation: 'Charcot, however, did *not* follow this path towards an explanation of hysteria [...].'[4] It is surprising because, in the standard rhetoric of obituaries, it is customary to trace the paths the deceased *did* follow. Freud admittedly continues by extolling in particular Charcot's attainments in the field of the exact description of symptoms and of precise diagnostic classification, and gives him the credit for being the first to describe male hysterical pathology. At one point, furthermore, he emphasizes that his mentor did indeed take a step that went beyond mere nosography, a step that 'assured him for all time, too, the fame of having been the first to explain hysteria': he had succeeded in artificially inducing hysterical paralyses in hypnotized patients and in proving 'that these paralyses were the result of ideas which had dominated the patient's brain at moments of a special disposition. In this way, the mechanism of a hysterical phenomenon was explained for the first time. This incomparably fine piece of clinical research was afterwards taken up by his own pupil, Pierre Janet, as well as Breuer and others, who developed from it a theory of neurosis [...]'.[5]

---

3  Freud 1893f: 19f.
4  Ibid.: 20 (my italics).
5  Ibid.: 22.

Astonishingly, Freud does not mention himself. What he had furnished by his somewhat convoluted description of the path that Charcot did *not* follow was in fact nothing other than a résumé of some of the main theses of the revolutionary 'Preliminary communication', which Breuer and he himself had published in the *Neurologisches Zentralblatt* with the title 'On the Psychical Mechanism of Hysterical Phenomena' in January 1893 – i.e. only a few months before the composition of the Charcot obituary – and which, some two years later, was to form the first chapter of the *Studies on Hysteria*. Freud later concisely summarized the main elements of their joint theory as follows:

> This asserted that hysterical symptoms arose when the affect of a mental process cathected with a strong affect was forcibly prevented from being worked over consciously in the normal way and was thus diverted into a wrong path. In cases of hysteria, according to this theory, the affect passed over into an unusual somatic innervation ('conversion'), but could be given another direction and got rid of ('abreacted'), if the experience were revived under hypnosis. The authors gave this procedure the name of 'catharsis' (purging, setting free of a strangulated affect).[6]

Even if Freud knew when he wrote the obituary that the downfall of Charcot's conception of hysteria was imminent, he nevertheless unreservedly admired his teacher's astounding capacity for clinical vision, which he appreciates in a much-quoted, unforgettable passage:

> He was not a reflective man, not a thinker: he had the nature of an artist – he was, as he himself said, a *'visuel'*, a man who sees. Here is what he himself told us about his method of working. He used to look again and again at the things he did not understand, to deepen his impression of them day by day, till suddenly an understanding of them dawned on him. [...]. He might be heard to say that the greatest satisfaction a man could have was to see something new – that is, to recognize it as new; and he remarked again and again on the difficulty and value of this kind of 'seeing'.[7]

Not long after his return from Paris, Freud had already acknowledged without the slightest reservation, in a letter to Carl Koller dated 13 October 1886, that with Charcot he had 'learned to see clinically' for the first time.[8]

---

6  Freud 1924f: 194.
7  Freud 1893f: 12.
8  Freud 1960a [1873-1939], new German edition 1968: 228.

Furthermore, it may already be added here that this training was indispensable to the genesis of *Studies on Hysteria* with its wealth of new visions and insights, now in the course of gestation.

## II

A hundred years have now elapsed since the publication in 1895 – probably in May[1] – of this primal book of psychoanalysis. Brought out by the publishing house of Franz Deuticke in Leipzig and Vienna, it had half-cloth binding with reinforced corners and was gold-blocked. However, a few rather differently bound copies of the first edition survive, which presumably owe their existence to the fact that in those days publishers would supply folded and gathered sheets to purchasers who wished to have their copies bound individually. At any rate, the text of all specimens is laid out identically in the classical typography used for scientific publications in the nineteenth century, set in narrow Antiqua. On the elegant title page,[2] playful serifs impart a graceful, decorative charm to the accentuated word 'Hysterie', while the delicate ornamental rule emphasizes the proportions of the Golden Section.

Franz Deuticke was then a young, enterprising scientific publisher. Within just a few years, he had succeeded in attracting as authors, in particular, numerous members of the widely renowned Vienna medical faculty. However, he had not only made a name for himself in the established university subjects, but had also added to his list new fields and topics of current interest, for example from the young social and economic sciences. Freud once called this agile-minded and dynamic entrepreneur, to whom he had already entrusted his monograph *On Aphasia* in 1891, his 'primal publisher'.[3]

It was not by chance that Deuticke gave special prominence to the word 'Hysterie' on the title page, because the book came out not in a vacuum but in the context of a well-structured publishing policy. Deuticke had a nose for important innovations and attentively observed the research on hysteria introduced by Charcot and his school, whose standard works he had brought out in German translation in quick succession. There were Charcot's *Leçons sur les maladies du système nerveux*, which had already appeared in Freud's German version in 1886, and his *Leçons du mardi à la*

---

1 As reported by Ernest Jones (1953: 252). I wish to thank Dr Eva Laible for her (unfortunately unsuccessful) attempt to verify the date in the Deuticke archives.
2 See the accompanying facsimile, Figure 1.
3 Freud 1963a [1909–39]: 58 (translation modified).

# STUDIEN

ÜBER

# HYSTERIE

VON

Dr. JOS. BREUER und Dr. SIGM. FREUD

IN WIEN.

———•———

LEIPZIG UND WIEN.
FRANZ DEUTICKE.
1895.

*Figure 1* Title page of the first edition of *Studien über Hysterie* (1895)

*Salpêtrière (1887–8)*, which, partly also translated by Freud, came on to the market in instalments between 1892 and 1894. Works by outstanding pupils of Charcot, too, were presented in Deuticke's list in 1894, namely the first volume of *Traité clinique et thérapeutique de l'hystérie d'après l'enseignement de la Salpêtrière* by Georges Gilles de la Tourette and Pierre Janet's *Etat mental des hystériques*. Before that, Deuticke had even offered his publishing house as a platform for Charcot's critic Hippolyte Bernheim; that had been in 1888–9, with the monograph *De la suggestion et de ses applications à la thérapeutique*, again partly translated by Freud, which had been followed in 1892, once more in Freud's German version, by the same author's *Hypnotisme, suggestion et psychothérapie, études nouvelles*.

The first edition of Breuer's and Freud's *Studies on Hysteria* comprised 800 copies. Almost fifteen years were to pass before the next printing in 1909; at any rate, no more than 626 copies are said to have been sold in thirteen years.[4] So the *Studies* shared the fate of many an innovative work that initially enjoyed only limited dissemination.

Yet its appearance cannot be said to have gone unnoticed by the specialist press at the time. A review was printed in the *Zeitschrift für Psychologie und Physiologie der Sinnesorgane* before the year of the book's publication was out.[5] Although his remarks were somewhat patronizing, the unsuspecting commentator nevertheless stressed the differences between the conceptions of Breuer and Freud and the teachings of the Charcot school, noting in particular the more thoroughgoing psychologization of the concept of hysteria, as compared with the French emphasis on heredity. It was indeed noteworthy that attention was first drawn to the *Studies* in a predominantly psychological journal, because the discipline of psychopathology was in those days still deemed an exclusively medical one.

In the following year, two leading scholars in the relevant field took up their pens. One was the renowned Erlangen neurologist Adolf von Strümpell and the other Eugen Bleuler, soon to become professor of psychiatry at the University of Zurich and Director of the Burghölzli sanatorium, who was later, as we know, for many years a champion of psychoanalysis. Strümpell began his review, published in the *Deutsche Zeitschrift für Nervenheilkunde*,[6] by noting that the book furnished gratifying evidence that the idea of the psychogenic nature of the symptoms of

---

4  Cf. Jones 1953: 253.

5  Vol. 10 (1895): 308–9. In his English-language compilation, Norman Kiell (1988) published a fairly large selection of reactions to *Studies on Hysteria* which includes most of the examples that now follow. However, all texts have been translated here from the original wording of the sources as quoted in the German version of this essay.

6  Vol. 8 (1896): 159–61.

hysterical pathology was gaining more and more ground among physicians. However, he then took issue with Breuer's theoretical chapter in particular, contending that its author had departed excessively from clinical empiricism. He had the following objection to a general application of the cathartic method: 'I do not know whether such a penetration into someone's most intimate private affairs may be deemed permissible even on the part of the most honourable doctor. I find this penetration most questionable where sexual matters are concerned [...].' He ended with the blunt assertion 'that just the same can be achieved by a sensible, direct psychic treatment without any hypnosis and without delving in too much detail into the "strangulated affect"'.[7] Eugen Bleuler, by contrast, began his review,[8] published in the *Münchener Medizinische Wochenschrift*, with a clear and detached exposition of the book's main theses. However, towards the end he did express doubts concerning the prevailing level of knowledge about hypnosis: the possibility could by no means be ruled out 'that the therapeutic successes of the "cathartic method" might be attributable not to the abreaction of a suppressed affect but simply to suggestion'. But Bleuler's final paragraph certainly betrays the fact that he had indeed understood something of the revolutionary character of the book, precisely in regard to its consequences for a *general* psychology of the unconscious: '[...] what the book actually contributes affords a completely new insight into the psychic mechanism and makes it one of the most important publications of the last few years in the field of normal or pathological psychology.'[9]

The first English-language appreciation also dates from 1896, when the work was the subject of a review in *Brain* whose approach was one of careful reporting rather than of judgement.[10] At the beginning and end, its author, the British neurologist and physician J. Mitchell Clarke, explicitly stressed that the *Studies* constituted an original and valuable contribution to contemporary research on hysteria, principally because they took so much account of the role of emotions in the causation of hysterical symptoms. As to the dialogue between physician and patient developed by Breuer and Freud, which was as intensive as it was intimate, the reviewer expressed similar misgivings to those of Strümpell and, in an objection comparable with Bleuler's, warned of the suggestibility of hysterical patients.

Among the reactions to the *Studies* in languages other than German, an essay by the English writer and researcher on sexuality, Henry Havelock Ellis, deserves particular mention, although it appeared only in 1898. In his

7 Ibid.: 160f.
8 Vol. 43 (1896): 524–5.
9 Ibid.: 525.
10 Vol. 19 (1896): 401–14.

conspectus of the history of views on the genesis of hysteria, entitled 'Hysteria in relation to the sexual emotions', the author ranges over the entire gamut of conceptions extending from the theory, which originated in Ancient Greece and prevailed for some two millennia, that the causative agent was the womb, which was said, in the bodies of women prevented from reproducing, to wander around in a state of unruly dissatisfaction – that is, pathogenically – to the revolutionary hypothesis of the seventeenth-century French physician Charles Lepois, who taught that the disease could occur at any age and in both sexes and that its seat was not in the uterus but in the brain – i.e. that it was a nervous illness. All the same, according to Ellis, modified versions of the womb theory, in which unsatisfied sexual emotions rather than the female generative organ itself were held responsible for the pathology, were still able to assert themselves until the middle of the nineteenth century. Only then did voices – first and foremost that of Pierre Briquet, a precursor of Charcot – begin to be heard which, not least in order to protect women from demeaning insinuations, strictly denied the existence of any connection between hysteria and the sexual aspects of life, whether physical or psychic. But it had been the genius of Charcot and the work of his pupils that had for the first time succeeded in forcing the theory of the sexual aetiology of hysteria into retreat, by rigorously insisting that the fundamental cause of this condition, as a *psychic* disturbance, should be sought in hereditary disposition.

However, Ellis himself recalls that, when he began to study hysteria, he could not avoid the impression that there was then a converse tendency to tone down the sexual factor impermissibly. At one point he makes the following noteworthy comment:

> Thus even a mainly *a priori* examination of the matter may lead us to see that many arguments still brought forward in favor of Charcot's position on this point fall to the ground when we realize that the sexual emotions in women (and the same is to some extent true of children and men) may constitute a highly complex psychic sphere, often hidden from observation, sometimes not conscious at all, and liable to many lesions besides that due to the non-satisfaction of sexual desire.[11]

Yet he stresses that it was incontrovertibly Charcot who, by his definition of hysteria as a *psychic* disturbance, pointed the way to its *psychological* investigation. As Ellis concedes, this path was followed first by Charcot's pupil Janet and then, in particular, by Breuer and Freud; moreover, in his trenchant and thorough essay, Ellis gives Freud most of the

---

11 Ellis 1898: 607.

credit for that revolutionary breakthrough, though he also takes account of the further writings on hysteria brought out by Freud soon after *Studies on Hysteria*.[12] Ellis sums up by praising the achievement of the two authors: '[...] they have supplied a definite psychic explanation of a psychic malady. They have succeeded in presenting clearly, at the expense of much labour, insight and sympathy, a dynamical view of the psychic processes involved in the constitution of the hysterical state [...].'[13] No wonder Freud gleefully welcomed Ellis's brilliant account in a letter to Wilhelm Fliess dated 3 January 1899, noting that Ellis was

> an author who [...] is obviously a highly intelligent man because his paper, which [...] deals with the connection between hysteria and sexual life, begins with Plato and ends with Freud; he agrees a great deal with the latter and gives Studies on Hysteria, as well as later papers, their due in a very sensible manner.[14]

In an earlier letter to his friend, written on 6 February 1896, Freud had already commented on the Strümpell review mentioned above, although in completely the opposite tone: 'Our book had a vicious review by Strümpell [...]; on the other hand, it was the subject of a very sensitive article by Freiherr von Berger in the old *Presse* on February 2, 1896.'[15] The reference is to another extraordinary appreciation, which appeared in the *Morgen-Presse* one Sunday. Under the headline 'Surgery of the Mind' and commencing in a prominent position on the front page, it for the first time drew the attention of the Viennese public at large to the outstanding importance of *Studies on Hysteria*. The epithet 'sensitive' should be taken literally, because the article's author, who was not a scientist but a literary man, had, with an incomparably more discriminating sensorium than that of the specialist reviewers, detected the specificity and radical novelty of Breuer's and Freud's work.

Alfred Freiherr[16] von Berger, Professor of the History of Literature at the University of Vienna and Director of the Burgtheater, himself refers at the beginning of his review to his own 'artistic receptivity, which [felt] stimulated and satisfied in many different ways by the content and form of

---

12 Freud 1896a and 1896c.
13 Ellis 1898: 614.
14 Freud 1985c [1887–1904]: 338.
15 Ibid.: 170 (translation slightly modified). Freud's reference to the old 'Presse' has misled a number of previous workers, who have looked in vain for the original wording there. The review has hitherto been quoted – as it is by Kiell – from the abbreviated reprint in the *Almanach der Psychoanalyse* for 1933. At my request, Eva Laible (Vienna) has now been able to identify the text in the *Morgen-Presse* and has kindly provided me with a copy.
16 Freiherr = Baron.

this book'. But he immediately concedes that the 'scholarly authors, with their strictly scientific minds, may deem this way of appropriating their book to oneself to be a curious abuse of the same. [...] They wanted to convey a piece of truth and to create something useful, not to write a beautiful book.' However, he also does not fail to quote Freud's famous dictum from the *Studies*: '[...] it still strikes me myself as strange that the case histories I write should read like short stories and that, as one might say, they lack the serious stamp of science. I must console myself with the reflection that the nature of the subject is evidently responsible for this, rather than any preference of my own.'[17]

Von Berger then attempts a more detailed description of this specific nature of the subject matter, anticipating some of the central ideas of Freud's later comparisons of analytic work with literary creation: 'He who wishes to plumb and describe the mental cannot completely escape the creative writer's methods of conceiving and describing, however rigorous the will to cool, sober objectivity.' Von Berger is as it were intuiting some fundamental principles of the mature psychoanalytic method, some of the consistent laws of empathy, or even countertransference in today's sense, when he observes: 'Yet mental processes, in which the innermost nerve of another's personality lies exposed, lure forth his own personality from whosoever ventures to engage with them, willy-nilly and wittingly or unwittingly. The latter betrays itself in the way he notices, feels with, understands and interprets the former. The most subtle fascination of the book lies perhaps herein.'

This perspicacious reviewer even realized that *Studies on Hysteria* had flung open the door to the scientific discovery of the unconscious internal world of man. Towards the end he writes:

> They appositely compare their method, whereby they expose one layer of memory after another, to the systematic excavation of a buried city. [...] We see in the case histories how the life impressions and memories are stored individually in a human being's mind, and we sense that it might one day be conceivable to lay our hands on the innermost secret of the individual personality. The life of a man impresses itself on his mind, upon which it confers the content that we call its character. Of this biography, about which he who has lived through it knows so little although he carries it with himself in his head and suffers from its consequences, the two physicians unwind at least a little piece, like a bandage, in order to decipher its content in the reverse order from that in which it was experienced and recorded.

---

17 Freud 1895d: 160.

### III

During the hundred years since the first publication of *Studies on Hysteria*, the work's significance came to be recognized only gradually. From the vantage point of today, it can be asserted with some justification that the book so to speak ushered in the century of psychotherapy, as the twentieth century, now drawing to a close, is sometimes called. The phrase 'Freudian century' may also be heard.

This is perhaps a good time to turn our attention to Josef Breuer. Although we have had little to say about him so far, it is impossible to imagine the beginnings of psychoanalysis without his rich, unassuming personality and his medical and intellectual originality. When Alfred von Berger in his review described the authors as 'two well-known, universally esteemed Vienna physicians', this characterization was in reality true only of the then fifty-four-year-old Breuer, who was indeed highly renowned as a family doctor specializing in internal medicine, but hardly of Freud, who was not yet quite forty and had been in private practice for a mere ten years. Freud had set up as a nerve specialist immediately after returning from his study trip to Paris in 1886 and had soon been confronted with the unedifying realization that little or nothing could be achieved in many of his neurotic patients with the treatments available at the time, namely electrotherapies, hydropathies, rest-cures, massage, and so on. Another study trip, this time to Nancy to perfect his hypnosis technique with Auguste Ambroise Liébeault and Hippolyte Bernheim, did not take him much further.

In this situation, his friendship and exchange of scientific ideas with Josef Breuer assumed renewed importance. The young Freud had already met Breuer, who was outstanding not only as a practitioner but also as a theoretician and experimental physiologist, in his university days at Ernst von Brücke's Physiological Institute. Breuer had become his friend and mentor, had helped him on in all kinds of ways and even rescued him from financial straits. Even before Freud went to Paris to study with Charcot in 1885, Breuer had informed him in detail of his unusual treatment of the severely hysterical 'Anna O.' between 1880 and 1882. Together with his highly gifted patient, the true discoverer of therapeutic reconstruction, Breuer had at that time developed the so-called cathartic method and, in countless conversations and encounters with her, obtained unexpected insights into the dynamics of mental pathology. In the course of this treatment, Breuer, unlike the Charcot school, had used hypnosis not for the purposes of crude behavioural suggestion but as a route to the memories of pathogenic traumatic experiences that were not accessible to the patient in the waking state. Looking back, Freud wrote in his obituary for Breuer in 1925:

> We psycho-analysts, who have long been familiar with the idea of devoting hundreds of sessions to a single patient, can form no conception of how novel such a procedure must have seemed forty-five years ago. It must have called for a large amount of personal interest and, if the phrase can be allowed, of medical libido, but also for a considerable degree of freedom of thought and certainty of judgement. At the date of the publication of our *Studies* we were able to appeal to Charcot's writings and to Pierre Janet's investigations, which had by that time deprived Breuer's discoveries of some of their priority. But when Breuer was treating his first case (in 1881–2) none of this was as yet available. [...] It seems that Breuer's researches were wholly original, and were directed only by the hints offered to him by the material of his case.[1]

The awareness of his therapeutic impotence seems to have reminded Freud of that early discussion about the case of Anna O.; the fact that he had thrust aside the memory of it for years suggests that he had resistances of his own to Breuer's findings. Driven so to speak by necessity, Freud now urged him to resume their former dialogue, even though Breuer for his part had by then stopped treating neuroses by the cathartic method. In a letter dated 21 November 1907 to Auguste Forel – who had presumably enquired about his share in *Studies on Hysteria* – Breuer later explained this retreat as follows:

> The main contribution that can be credited to me is that I recognized what an enormously instructive, scientifically important case chance had assigned to me for treatment, and that I persevered in attentive and faithful observation and did not disturb the simple apprehension of the important facts with preconceived notions. In this way I at that time

---

1 Freud 1925g: 279f. But cf. p. 15, n. 2 on the earlier publications of Azam, whose own studies of the case of Félida X, in which he also involved her husband, likewise extended over a long period. However, Azam's main interest lay in research on the physiology of the brain and on psychology rather than, as yet, directly in therapy, which he saw as a distant goal: 'J'ai la confiance que l'analyse bien faite des futurs faits de cet ordre perfectionnera leur thérapeutique. Ce désir n'est pas superflu, car il faut reconnaître que le traitement des accidents de cette nature est entouré d'un vague qui laisse une prise déplorable au charlatanisme de tout genre' ['I am confident that the proper analysis of future facts of this nature will lead to the perfecting of their therapy. That is not asking too much, for it must be acknowledged that the treatment of such accidents is surrounded by an aura of insubstantiality which affords a regrettable purchase to quackery of every kind'] (1877: 581). Freud was incidentally acquainted with Azam's observations (cf. 1912g: 263).

learned a great deal – much that was of scientific value, but also the important practical lesson that it is impossible for a 'general practitioner'[2] to treat such a case without his activity and the conduct of his life thereby being completely ruined. I vowed at the time *never* again to subject myself to such an ordeal.[3] So when cases came to me where I expected much from analytical treatment, but which I could not myself treat, I referred them to Dr Freud, who had come from Paris and the Salpêtrière and with whom I entertained the most intimate relations of friendship and scientific communication.[4]

At least with the first patient he treated by the cathartic method, 'Frau Emmy von N.', Freud was thus to some extent working under Breuer's supervision; as can be seen from the *Studies*, Breuer occasionally even involved himself directly in the various medical interventions. Whereas Breuer had decided, as far as the empirical practice of analysis was concerned, that enough was enough following his once-for-all observations in the case of Anna O., Freud for his part developed over a number of years into an increasingly experienced psychotherapist. In the process, he also gradually modified the therapeutic technique, abandoning Breuer's method in favour of his own concentration or pressure procedure. He made less and less use of hypnosis and, increasing the patient's freedom, confined the element of suggestion to assuring her that if she would but concentrate, the memories relevant to her suffering would surely come. He lent emphasis to his assurance by brief and occasionally repeated body contact, in the form of pressure of his hand on the patient's forehead. At any rate, it was Freud who, in direct analytic confrontation with the patients in the field, gathered the material for the scientific discourse with Breuer.

It had plainly not been difficult to induce Breuer to reactivate the ideas he had elaborated in the past during the treatment of Anna O. As the letter quoted above shows, he himself had at the time been fully convinced of their innovative significance, but the infectious verve and enthusiasm of the youthful Freud seem to have been necessary for them to be recathected and introduced into a high-powered, topical research dialogue. The revolutionary results of this dialogue are recorded in the joint publications, the 'Preliminary communication' of 1893 and, precisely, the *Studies on Hysteria* of 1895; however, traces of the two men's inspiring cooperation can also be found in Freud's posthumously published letters to Wilhelm

---

2 'General practitioner' in English in the original.
3 'Ordeal' in English in the original.
4 Ackerknecht 1957: 170.

Fliess and in both published and unpublished notes and draft manuscripts dating from the time of their collaboration. The fact that Breuer was by no means a mere passenger in the process, but saw himself as an active partner with equal status, is evident, for example, from a comment subsequently preserved for posterity in Freud's obituary; in connection with the preparations for the publication of their joint book, Breuer had once remarked: 'I believe [...] that this is the most important thing we two have to give the world.'[5]

IV

Let us now turn to *Studies on Hysteria* itself. The primal book of psychoanalysis has, over the years, given rise to a flood of secondary literature. For example, newly discovered documents have dragged its *dramatis personae* – those heroic and indeed almost mythical female patients from the prehistory and dawn of psychoanalysis – out from behind their poetic pseudonyms and identified them; the subsequent history of their lives, successes and suffering has been traced and in some cases the patients have been rediagnosed[1] and re-treated in imagination. These publications cover an enormously diverse range and cannot be appreciated individually here.[2] The reader is invited instead to turn direct to the text of the *Studies* itself, and simply to read or reread it spontaneously. The following five selected, overlapping themes are intended to encourage such a reading:

---

5  Freud 1925g: 280. For more details, cf. the authoritative monograph on Breuer by A. Hirschmüller (1989) [1978].

---

1  A more careful reading of the *Studies* would have rendered superfluous such rediagnosis, in which the patients are classified, for example, as schizophrenics or borderlines. The authors are in fact found to keep their diagnostic considerations flexible. They refer to a 'mixed' disorder (e.g. 138); while Freud, in a nosological passage in his final chapter, explicitly points out 'that it was not right to stamp a neurosis as a whole as hysterical because a few hysterical signs were prominent in its complex of symptoms' (258). Again: 'The neuroses which commonly occur are mostly to be described as "mixed"' (259). Finally, he illustrates this contention with examples relating to the five main protagonists. Precisely this lack of preconception, an attitude in which, for instance, the phenomenon of change of symptom is perceived and taken seriously, was recently described by Stavros Mentzos as an astonishingly modern feature of the *Studies*: 'Hysteria [is regarded] more as a pattern of reaction and less (as was later the case) as a nosological entity [or] mode of working over the conflict' (1991: 18).

2  For a general survey, cf. Micale 1989. This paper contains not only an appreciation of a variety of 'retrospective rediagnoses' of the patients featuring in the *Studies*, but also a comprehensive interdisciplinary account of the historiography of hysteria, extending from the history of ideas via the history of the Charcot school and of psychoanalysis to feminist studies and research on the political and social context.

seeing and hearing; modification of the doctor–patient relationship; form of reporting; seeds of psychoanalytic theory; and prototypes of psycho-analytic technique. And if the reader applies himself to Charcot's art of 'seeing', he may sometimes experience the promised 'greatest satisfaction' in which it is vouchsafed to him 'to see something new' – in this case, in the encounter with a supposedly thoroughly familiar classical text.

It is indeed worthwhile, in considering both the major case histories and the book's short vignettes, to study not only the 'seeing' of the two doctors and the precision with which the visible symptoms are observed, but also the varied range of gesture and facial expression displayed by the patients. Indeed, in his concluding chapter on psychotherapy, Freud explicitly recommends that, in deciding whether it is really the case that no memory occurs to the patient or whether she is withholding something for defensive reasons, the physician should never lose sight of the play of the patient's features as she lies quietly on the couch. Yet this specific way of 'seeing' still preserves a distance between patient and therapist and keeps the observed strictly separate from the observer.

In this respect, matters had been no different with Charcot. In the contribution mentioned above, Havelock Ellis gave a highly impressive account of the paradoxical situation of the great Frenchman, who, although he had identified hysteria as a psychic illness, was simply averse to psychological investigation.[3] Ellis notes that anyone who had the privilege of witnessing the Napoleonic figure, with its haughtily contemptuous and sometimes ill-humoured mien, at the Salpêtrière clinical demonstrations could not fail to realize this:

> The questions addressed to the patient were cold, distant, sometimes impatient; Charcot clearly had little faith in the value of any results so obtained. One may well believe also, that a man whose superficial personality was so haughty and awe-inspiring to strangers, would in any case have had the greatest difficulty in penetrating the mysteries of a psychic world so obscure and elusive as that presented by the hysterical.[4]

There can be no doubt that the radical revolutionization of clinical perception was fully accomplished only when 'hearing' too came to be

---

3  As Freud himself was to stress in a letter to Ernest Jones written in 1928: 'Charcot had no interest in a psychological study of hysteria' (Freud 1993e [1908–39]: 653).
4  Ellis 1898: 608.

incorporated in the perceptual process. Pierre Janet seems to have paved the way for this new orientation, for example when, notwithstanding his otherwise quasi-experimental attitude to patients, he writes at the beginning of his book *Etat mental des hystériques* that 'il faut avant tout bien connaître son sujet dans sa vie, dans son éducation, dans ses idées [...]. [...] et je trouve ni inutile ni fastidieux d'écrire *mot à mot* les divagations d'une aliénée' ['above all one must be thoroughly acquainted with the subject in respect of his life, education, character and ideas {...}. {...} and I find it neither useless nor irksome to write down *word for word* the ramblings of a lunatic woman'].[5] The process of learning to hear may conceivably have been prepared for, in Freud, by the interest in matters acoustic forced upon him by his earlier research on aphasia.[6]

Listening so intensively and patiently to the person being treated, whatever she had to say, was tantamount to admitting her inside oneself, allowing her to come into contact with one's inmost being – or, in present-day terms, exposing one's own unconscious to the onslaught of that of the other, with all the associated risks of psychic destabilization. This also signified an unprecedented heightening of intimacy between the two protagonists; it is not for nothing that Josef Breuer averred that the life of Anna O. 'became known to me to an extent to which one person's life is seldom known to another'.[7] Again, although these manifestations are of course not yet formulated as 'self-analysis' or 'countertransference', countless passages in the *Studies* could be identified in which the recording and observation of the therapist's own psychic impulses and processes are utilized in their work; this is true of both authors. In other words, the scandalous permeabilization of the traditional distinction between normality and pathology starts already here.

The new kind of listening at the same time turned the spotlight on language and opened up the entire semantic dimension, that of the highly differentiated, word-related understanding of the other's psyche. Listening was even directed to language itself. This is the case, for example, when Breuer opens his ears to the sense of phrases such as '"to cry oneself out" [or] "to blow off steam"';[8] or when Freud, as it were practising psychosomatic thinking, writes the following about his hysterical patient:

---

5  Janet n.d. [1894?]: 3 (my italics).
6  Freud 1891b.
7  Freud 1895d: 21f.
8  Ibid.: 202.

In taking a verbal expression literally and in feeling the 'stab in the heart' or the 'slap in the face' after some slighting remark as a real event, the hysteric is not taking liberties with words, but is simply reviving once more the sensations to which the verbal expression owes its justification. How has it come about that we speak of someone who has been slighted as being 'stabbed to the heart' unless the slight had in fact been accompanied by a precordial sensation which could suitably be described in that phrase and unless it was identifiable by that sensation?[9]

Perhaps this invention of the art of listening was facilitated by the fact that the disturbances afflicting some of the early patients – in particular, Anna O. and Frau Emmy von N. – pre-eminently concerned the function of speech, so that the customary precise study of symptoms positively demanded a new kind of auditory approach.[10] If the authors wanted to understand the significance of the loss of conjugation, the garnering of words from several foreign languages, and indeed the process of 'translation' in Anna O.'s symptomatology, or what lay behind Emmy von N.'s stereotyped protective formula 'Keep still! – Don't say anything! – Don't touch me!', they first had to develop a keen ear for the stratum-by-stratum revelation of the grammar of emotionally charged memories of traumatic experiences.

Narration took centre stage in the treatment. One of the objects of the therapist's listening was the symptoms 'joining in the conversation'; however, symptoms were also 'talked through' and 'talked away'. What then emerged were not primarily case histories but highly specific biographies; not carriers of symptoms or even hereditary defects, but people, girls and women. We meet the following unique figures: *Anna O.*, the bourgeois 'girl [...] bubbling over with intellectual vitality'[11] and goodness, hungry for emancipation, victim of her two selves, in one of which she was sad and anxious and in the other scolding, with a tendency to throw cushions at people, the inventor of the 'talking cure'; *Frau Emmy von N.*, the widowed estate owner who made a clacking noise like the call of a capercaillie, an unruly shrew of a woman who was justifiably quick to take fright; *Miss Lucy R.*, the laconic English governess with the olfactory sensation of burnt pudding and the repressed love for her employer, who resigned herself after the relevant interpretation to the fact that her wishes could never be fulfilled; *Katharina*, the decent country girl subjected to

---

9 Ibid.: 181.
10 The prominence of disturbances of speech in the symptomatology of hysterical patients is, incidentally, already evident in the vignettes of Janet (n.d. [1894?]).
11 Freud 1895d: 22.

sexual harassment by her father,[12] with her sulky-looking face and shortness of breath, with whom Freud found it 'so much easier [...] to talk [...] than to the prudish ladies'[13] of his city practice; *Fräulein Elisabeth von R.*, the highly intelligent, high-ranking lady from Hungary whose ambition was matched only by her craving for love, suffering from seemingly indeterminate leg pains, cunningly and triumphantly resisting every attempt to forge a connection between her suffering and its history. These are the five main protagonists. No less colourful and specific are the figures sketched in the vignettes and their destinies – in particular, the inspiring *Cäcilie M.*, whom Freud once called his 'teacher',[14] whose case history could not be reported in detail owing to 'personal considerations' – as well as *Mathilde H.*, *Rosalia H.* and the many others not given prominence by pseudonyms of their own.

With four or five exceptions, these numerous patients described in passing, mostly in footnotes, are also women and girls. The statement that hysteria was at the time considered to be a pre-eminently feminine disease does not adequately explain the striking imbalance in its distribution between the sexes. It is conceivable that the new way of seeing and hearing was more fascinating and productive when applied to *female* patients because women are usually closer to their own emotionality and corporality and because it was more socially acceptable for them to live out the inventive, mobile aspects of the hysterical object relationship.[15]

---

12 The text, however, describes him as the girl's uncle. Freud did not disclose the true relationship until he added a footnote in 1924 for the reprint of the *Studies* in the *Gesammelte Schriften*: 'I venture after the lapse of so many years to lift the veil of discretion and reveal the fact that Katharina was not the niece but the daughter of the landlady. The girl fell ill, therefore, as a result of sexual attempts on the part of her own father. Distortions like the one which I introduced in the present instance should be altogether avoided in reporting a case history. From the point of view of understanding the case, a distortion of this kind is not, of course, a matter of such indifference as would be the shifting of the scene from one mountain to another' (1895d: 134, n. 2). Until then, Freud had hinted at the true relationship only at the end of the very first paragraph of the case history, at the point where, in the description of his initial meeting with Katharina, he conjectures in passing that she must 'no doubt be a daughter or relative of the landlady's' (ibid.: 125). It may be noted that Freud's distortion, while it increases the relational distance between Katharina and her father, also differs from the actual situation by describing a consummated incest, which even results in a pregnancy, between the fictitious uncle and his fictitious daughter Franziska.

13 Ibid.: 132.

14 Freud 1985c [1887–1904]: 229.

15 This last point seems to be borne out by a passage from Janet's book *Etat mental des hystériques* (n.d. [1894?]: 223):

On a souvent signalé une distinction assez juste entre l'hystérie de l'homme et celle de la femme. On représente la femme hystérique comme agitée, remuante, gaie, riant

When doctors were finally prepared to listen, it seems that these patients became spontaneously capable of speaking. The book contains not a few passages where the two authors express their gratitude to their creative female partners in the process of research.

Of course, this hearing, this speaking and this invention of a new form of therapeutic dialogue implied a fundamental change in the traditional doctor–patient relationship. Admitting the possibility that patients had anything to say at all, that their symptoms conveyed a concealed meaning about which, albeit not yet available or capable of being recalled to memory, the subject certainly 'knew' more than the physician in charge, who therefore had to learn to tolerate his ignorance – all this diminished the customary authoritarian gradient between one party who was potentially omniscient and another who was the mere passive recipient of prescriptions. The opening up of a space in which the patient could express and portray herself was revealed if only by the unusual temporal intensity of the medical attention devoted to her. The impression is sometimes gained from reading the case histories that Breuer and Freud positively lived with their patients, or at any rate on occasion saw and spoke to them several times a day, not only in the consulting room but also in their domestic surroundings. Freud does concede that the 'procedure is laborious and time-consuming for the physician [...]'. He goes on: 'I cannot imagine bringing myself to delve into the psychical

---

aux éclats, faisant mille folies, et l'homme, au contraire, comme plus triste, plus mélancolique et inerte. Les choses se présentent le plus communément de cette manière, et il est certain que l'hystérie de l'homme, 'ce renversement des lois constitutives de la société', selon Briquet, est plus pénible, plus cruelle que celle de la femme. Un homme souffre plus de cette inertie, de cette destruction de toute force vive, et son affaiblissement moral étonne davantage.

Mais, derrière cette différence apparente, il y a un fond de ressemblance, et l'hystérie est toujours la même. C'est la mélancolie et la tristesse qui sont les sentiments dominants chez les femmes comme chez les hommes.

[Attention has often been drawn to a highly pertinent distinction between male and female hysteria. One imagines the hysterical woman as excited, restless, cheerful, full of noisy laughter and inclined to every folly, but the hysterical man, by contrast, rather as sad, gloomy and lethargic. On the whole, that is indeed the case, and there can be no doubt that male hysteria – 'that overturning of the constitutive laws of society', as Briquet puts it – is much more distressing and cruel than its female counterpart. A man suffers more from this inertia and destruction of all his vigour, and his moral enfeeblement is more surprising.

Behind this seeming difference, however, lies a basis of similarity, and hysteria is always the same. Melancholy and sadness are the predominant feelings in women and men alike].

mechanism of a hysteria in anyone who struck me as low-minded and repellent'.[16]

It is evident from the book that this abandonment of the privileged position of the doctor confronted both investigators with an acute dilemma. The gradual consolidation of the new attitude can be traced chronologically in Freud's case histories. In the earliest treatment, that of Frau Emmy von N., the patient's body is still involved in a literally hands-on form of total therapy, for example in the form of the application of a faradic brush to her anaesthetic leg, whole-body massage performed by Freud himself, or directions concerning what she was to eat and drink. Nor, in his hypnotic suggestions, did Freud shun 'white' lies and tricks; at this stage, a free space for the patient to reflect, express herself and contradict the doctor seems to be guaranteed at most in the conversations in the waking state. Such lapses into the traditional authoritarian manners of a physician are lacking in the conversation Freud had some four years later with Katharina while holidaying in the mountains. Here he dispenses with the most direct psychotherapeutic instrument of power, namely hypnosis, and, where necessary, encourages the young girl seeking his help to cooperate by occasional discreet questioning: a simple 'Well?' to spur her on, or the courteous interjection: 'Fräulein Katharina, if you could remember now what was happening in you at that time [...].'[17]

The dilemma also extended to the listening itself. The two researchers were not always in the mood for patient waiting. They would then interrupt, exert pressure, and curtail their ignorance by peremptory assertions, but a little later call themselves to order and again display a willingness to learn: 'I now saw,' Freud admonishes himself, 'that I had gained nothing by this interruption and that I cannot evade listening to her stories in every detail to the very end'.[18] So he had to keep an ear open to the criticism of the grumbling Emmy von N. when she complained 'that I was not to keep on asking her where this and that came from, but to let her tell me what she had to say'.[19]

Even the attitude to the patients as human beings fluctuates: unusual respect, recognition and even admiration for their personality, moral and intellectual fibre, strength of will, working energy and realism hold sway for long periods, only to be interrupted by sudden countervailing tendencies. Examples are when Freud speaks of the 'discipline'[20] into

---

16 Freud 1895d: 265.
17 Ibid.: 128.
18 Ibid.: 61.
19 Ibid.: 63.
20 Ibid.: 160 (translation modified; in the *Standard Edition* Freud's word 'Zucht' is rendered inadequately by 'care').

which he has taken Fräulein Elisabeth von R., or when Breuer, craving indulgence for the sheer bulk of the Anna O. case history, uses a distancing comparison:

> It was, however, impossible to describe the case without entering into details, and its features seem to me of sufficient importance to excuse this extensive report. In just the same way, the eggs of the echinoderm are important in embryology, not because the sea-urchin is a particularly interesting animal but because the protoplasm of its eggs is transparent and because what we observe in them thus throws light on the probable course of events in eggs whose protoplasm is opaque.[21]

Nowadays it is occasionally objected that the patients in the *Studies* were inadequately understood and treated. Freud at least, as we know, later took precisely this view. He wrote in a letter dated 13 July 1918 to the daughter of Emmy von N.: 'But kindly bear in mind that at that time [...] I did not understand anything about the case of your mother'.[22] Such know-it-all criticism betrays, if nothing else, a lack of imagination about what it meant to allow one's own internal world to come into contact for the first time with the unconscious mental life of a disturbed human being without being equipped for this by the fully developed theory of psychoanalysis and its therapeutic technique. So when Breuer and Freud lapsed into the traditional domineering style of dealing with neurotic patients, one reason was presumably in order to allay, at least temporarily, *their own* archaic anxieties.

However, *Studies on Hysteria* not only presents a new approach to clinical seeing and hearing and a new kind of doctor–patient relationship, but also features a novel form of description. The protraction and intensity of the treatments are reflected in comparatively long case histories replete with minute detail, whose purported overexactitude the authors actually felt it incumbent upon themselves to justify again and again. When Breuer and Freud encountered patients as personalities in their undiminished singularity and subjectivity, they were compelled so to speak to portray them in the manner of a painter. 'This lady, when I first saw her, was lying on a sofa with her head resting on a leather cushion. She still looked young and had finely-cut features, full of character':[23] so, somewhat unusually for

---

21 Ibid.: 41.
22 Bauer 1986: 97.
23 Freud 1895d: 48.

a traditional case report, begins Freud's account, in which he not only describes his own first meeting with Emmy von N., but at the same time allows the reader to see her. Again, the frequent use by both authors of direct speech, with the original German text sometimes even reproducing dialect, makes us witnesses of the new listening. We ourselves can hear the patients speak without any mediation; this authenticity of rendering is also to be found in Freud's surviving notes. Direct speech is often used, too, to describe the doctor–patient dialogue, so that we are drawn into the work of discovery as it proceeds and can share the feeling of evidence that ultimately arises.[24] At any rate, the authors were seeking an appropriate way of conveying something that had never been described before, namely the process character of the freshly tested analytic work.

The *Studies* are made up of four parts, of which three are predominantly theoretical in nature and one, comprising five case histories, is clinical; the case reports as a whole take up rather more space than the theoretical sections combined. The book begins with a reprint of the old 'Preliminary communication', 'On the psychical mechanism of hysterical phenomena', composed jointly by both authors in spite of their differences, so to speak at the end of the golden age of their cooperation. This text is in effect the vinculum that holds the entire work together, and so both Breuer and Freud refer to it again and again in their individual parts, composed under the shadow of their incipient alienation. As the preface has it, the 'Preliminary communication' presents 'as concisely as possible the theoretical conclusions'[25] to which they had come at the time. It is surely no coincidence that it is reproduced unchanged in its original form – that is to say, that the authors passed up the opportunity to adapt the wording to the context of the book, for example by deleting overlaps with the case material mentioned or replacing them by cross-references.

Yet the theoretical and clinical parts of the *Studies* are not as categorically distinct from each other as first impressions might suggest. Just as the theoretical sections are broken up and illustrated again and again by

---

24 As it happens, Azam (cf. p. 15, n. 2) had already adopted the practice of using direct speech to reproduce the words of the patient Félida X and his dialogues with her (e.g. 1876a: 483 and 485; 1877: 577). Janet too had aimed at this form of authenticity: 'Le lecteur ne sera donc pas étonné s'il m'arrive [...] de citer une phrase prononcée ou écrite par une malade. Les paroles, les écrits des malades sont les véritables documents, les graphiques de la psychologie pathologique' ['The reader will therefore not be surprised if I find myself in the position {...} of quoting a sentence spoken or written by a patient. Patients' words and writings are the true documents, the graphic proofs, of pathological psychology'] (n.d. [1894?]: 3).
25 Freud 1895d: xxix.

vignettes, so the case histories, brim-full of clinical material as they are, contain a plethora of theoretical considerations and digressions, not only in the epicrises but also in the ongoing narration of the case reports themselves. Freud, however, does his best not to interrupt the linearity – or 'chronicle' – of the treatment process, preferring to add his theoretical considerations, whether contemporaneous or subsequent, in the form of interpolated remarks or footnotes. This interpenetration of theory and clinical description characterizes in particular the final chapter on therapeutic theory, concerning which Freud himself says that much 'of the substance of this is already contained in the case histories printed in the earlier portion of this book'.[26]

The case histories – which are literally *histories*; the reader will see that Freud, as quoted earlier, was justified in noting that they 'read like short stories' – are of bewildering diversity. They reflect not only the differences between the two authors' ways of looking and listening and, in Freud's case, the rapid evolution of his therapeutic technique and manner of reporting, but also the worlds of difference between the personalities, life histories and social origins of the five protagonists. All these distinctions – and not only the traditional ones between symptoms and between responses to the relevant medical measures – were significant and the intention was that they should be able to reveal themselves.

Admittedly, Breuer's classical portrayal of his treatment of Anna O., Bertha Pappenheim, who later became famous for her social and professional achievements, still shows vestiges of the orthodox medical case-report style. Questions of hereditary disposition are discussed and the contributions of contemporary workers on hysteria appreciated; the conspicuous distance between the dramatic, strenuous, tormented suffering of the patient and Breuer's calm, mature depiction seems to accentuate the separateness of observer and observed. However, between the lines the reader does sense the extent to which Breuer clung to the 'great inner logic'[27] of the data supplied by his patient, in order not to lose himself in the 'ordeal' of that exorbitant treatment. Many passages betray the underlying ideal that the successive revelation of the traumatic memories should be totally complete, and this too may have had a structuring effect.[28]

---

26 Ibid.: 255.
27 Ibid.: 43 (translation modified; the *Standard Edition* uses the phrase 'such a degree of internal consistency').
28 According to later reconstructions, incidentally, Breuer referred to the 'final cure of the hysteria' (Freud 1895d: 47) although he knew that the patient was by no means well after the ending of the treatment. Of the authors writing subsequently to the researches of Henry F. Ellenberger (1970, 1972), cf. in particular Hirschmüller (1989 [1978]: 116).

To judge from his first and longest case history, 'Frau Emmy von N., age 40, from Livonia', Freud at first shared this perfectionist ideal. At any rate, there are recurring self-reproaches concerning the fragmentary and superficial nature of his own work. Indeed, the report seems to be characterized by a quasi-adolescent alternation between shamefaced apology and assertiveness – perhaps an honest, unembellished and unconcealed reflection, unusual for medical communications of the time, of the author's own inexperience and inadequacy. Reading this oddly rough-hewn case history, we participate directly in the experience of Freud, as the junior partner and beginner in analysis, of being overtaxed by this powerful, well-to-do patient, who was a kind of pre-'Wolf Man'. Down to its very linguistic structures, it is the description of a therapeutic *struggle*. The present-day reader will not be surprised that this difficult transference/counter-transference entanglement, which, of course, could not be understood as such at the time, proved unresolvable and ended in a manner that was hardly flattering to Freud. The clarity of the epicrisis indicates what a relief it must have been to him to be able, subsequently at least, to stem the chaos through the strength of his theoretical thinking.

Freud does not explain why he followed the case history of Emmy by the reports on Miss Lucy R. and Katharina instead of adopting chronological order and presenting next the clinical description of Fräulein Elisabeth von R., the subject of his first – in his opinion – complete analysis. Whereas his clinical aim with Emmy had still been to apply Breuer's cathartic method as correctly as possible, he treated Lucy without hypnosis by the pressure technique he was gradually evolving; the case history, which is perhaps also the finest illustration of the accomplishment of the therapeutic aim of 'transforming [...] hysterical misery into common unhappiness',[29] does indeed contain the first description of this new method. Possibly he wanted to demonstrate some independence already here, not yet half-way through the book. But he may also have had compositional reasons for sandwiching the two short, linear accounts of his successful efforts with a couple of unsophisticated women of the people who wished to recover between the pair of long, labyrinthine case histories of two convoluted, highly educated, upper-class personalities.

That said, the description of his encounter with Katharina is not really a case history at all, but as it were the first innovative record of an initial consultation,[30] a miniature painted with gentle dabs of the brush, intended to convey an impression of the effectiveness of analytic seeing and hearing

---

29 Freud 1895d: 305.
30 Cf. Argelander 1976.

even away from the consulting room, 'with a simple talk'.[31] The clinical description of 'Fräulein Elisabeth von R.' in fact occupies a midway position. The case history itself, spare and transparent as it is, building up to a thrilling climax almost in the manner of a detective story, is perhaps the most masterly of all. Although at the end it looks for a few moments as if the treatment has failed, the outcome, unlike that in the case of Emmy, is ultimately good; the complexity here lies in an unusually expanded epicrisis, which includes a number of additional vignettes and, taken as a whole, is almost as long as the case history proper, while sometimes diverging substantially from it in content. Then comes Breuer's extended chapter 'Theoretical'; could it be that, in this unconventionally luxuriant epicrisis, Freud was at the same time formulating 'his own' theoretical chapter, placing it before Breuer's exposition?[32]

What is certain is that the two authors, now writing separately, are each already going their own ways in their respective theoretical final chapters – Breuer in 'Theoretical' and Freud in 'The psychotherapy of hysteria' – even if they constantly mention each other: Breuer, who has long since turned away from psychotherapeutic work, in retrospective mood gives rein to some highly speculative ideas[33] that take him closer to physiology again; while Freud, looking forward and arguing 'principally under my own name',[34] is essentially concerned with the further development of the instruments of therapeutic technique that might open wider the door to the unconscious internal world and hence to his life-work.

Against the background of these two great texts, let us now discuss the extent to which *Studies on Hysteria* can indeed justifiably be called the

---

31  Freud 1895d: 127.
32  Albrecht Hirschmüller conjectures (1989 [1978]: 163f.) that the 'Project for a scientific psychology' (Freud 1950c [1895]) contains Freud's reply to Breuer's 'Theoretical'.
33  When I asked Prof. Wolf Singer, Director of the Max Planck Institute of Brain Research in Frankfurt, for a modern brain researcher's reaction to section 2, on intracerebral tonic excitations, he kindly replied as follows:

> [...] in the highest degree fascinating. Almost everything formulated there as mere suspicion and with gratifying circumspection has since been confirmed experimentally. This is all the more surprising if it is borne in mind that Breuer could not then have known anything about the existence of the ARAS – the ascending reticular activation system – and that no one knew that nerve cells function as switching elements in the brain or that electrical excitability serves as the signal carrier for processing operations. In reading through the chapter, I was tempted to substitute the accepted modern technical terms for Breuer's analogy-based concepts.

34  Freud 1895d: 256.

'primal book of psychoanalysis', and consider which of the fundamental elements of psychoanalytic theory and technique are already preformulated therein and which are lacking.

The term 'psychoanalysis' itself admittedly does not yet occur; as we know, Freud did not introduce it until a year later.[35] Although only the words 'analysis' and 'analytical' occur, there is no overlooking the fact that genuinely psychoanalytic terms and concepts are present in the work. The contrasting of conscious and unconscious ideas, of what the 'unsuspecting' consciousness[36] has at its disposal with what is stored in the knowing *unconscious*, as well as the description of the *dynamic* play of forces between these two spheres of the psyche, are certainly basic themes of the book, developed on the basis of a theoretical inkling of the role of *psychic conflict*. This is directly connected with the substantially advanced examination of the mechanism of *repression*, and indeed of *defence* in general. Although the emphasis in the aetiological considerations is still on *trauma*, the involvement of *drive*-related factors may already be discerned in a number of places, and even the term *sexual drive* occurs. Encouraged by their reflections on the hypnotized state, the authors draw attention again and again to *dreams* and the analogy between them and psychosis. In other words, the characteristic claim to be made by the future discipline of psychoanalysis, to be a psychology of both normal and pathological mental life, is here staked out.

Investigation of the mechanisms of *symptom formation*, and in particular of *conversion*, is one of the authors' central objectives, for which purpose they focus on the *symbolic relationship* between the traumatic experience responsible for the symptom, on the one hand, and the symptom itself in the form it ultimately takes, as a 'mnemic symptom' or 'mnemic symbol', on the other. Even if certain subsequent psychoanalytic concepts do not yet always appear in their definitive terminology, we come across preliminary formulations of, for example, *cathexis*, the *economic point of view*, the *primary and secondary processes*, *overdetermination*, *deferred action* [Nachträglichkeit], *somatic compliance*, *false connection*, *censorship*, the *parapraxis*, the *daydream*, the *day's residues* and *mourning-work*.

The main element lacking is insight into the significance of the early-infantile and infantile phases of life for the configuring of the internal world and of the pathological process of neurosis – in particular, the concept of the Oedipus complex and an appreciation of the importance of pre-Oedipal and Oedipal infantile sexual development and phantasies.

---

35 Cf. Freud 1896a, 1896b.
36 Freud 1895d: 76, n. 1.

'Quite frequently it is some event in childhood that sets up a more or less severe symptom which persists during the years that follow': this particular comment from the 'Preliminary communication',[37] several descriptions of incestuous factors in the case histories and an incidental comparison of the motor phenomena of hysterical attacks with young babies kicking about and waving their arms and legs,[38] do indeed give not the slightest indication of the huge areas of the continent represented by the internal world – 'psychic reality' in the strict sense of the term – still to be discovered after the publication of the *Studies*.

As regards the treatment technique used, one is likely to be surprised yet again to find that the two most pre-eminently 'analytic' forms – Breuer's cathartic method and Freud's technique of concentration and/or pressure – arose out of the therapeutic process; they were at any rate not something the two men had thought up outside the clinical situation and independently of the patients' collaboration. Both versions of the technique are embedded in a curious hotchpotch of diverse therapeutic measures. Apart from the traditional measures applied to the body by any general practitioner, and active interventions in the shaping of the patients' everyday lives, the psychotherapeutic factors proper, seen from the vantage point of today, include aspects not only of analysis but also of behaviour, family or *Gestalt* therapy. One example is when Freud sends Elisabeth von R. to visit her sister's grave or involves members of her family, with a view to evoking further revealing memories; another occurs in Breuer's treatment of Anna O., when her mother's diary is called upon to confirm reconstructions or the patient tries to reproduce an aetiologically important anxiety hallucination 'by the help of re-arranging the room so as to resemble her father's sickroom'.[39]

Yet, in the midst of this tangle of suggestive and intrusive interventions, seeds of classical psychoanalytic technique can be discerned. The less recourse was had to hypnosis and suggestion, the more the attitude of patient listening – as a preliminary form of *evenly suspended attention* – was consolidated, and, concomitantly, the more significant the subject's speaking in the waking state became, the more frequently and clearly these seeds emerged. The women being treated are no longer put under pressure, but are as it were invited to ally themselves with the therapist in a

---

37 Ibid.: 4.
38 Ibid.: 15.
39 Ibid.: 40.

state of not-yet-knowing; indeed, their curiosity about the joint analytic investigative process is aroused. Although the terms themselves again do not appear, there are passages that read like a description of the *working alliance* or of *working-through*. Furthermore, it is the patients themselves who occasionally demonstrate directly the productivity of *free association*, even if this has not yet been truly recognized, let alone conceptualized in theory. Many a cautious direction by Breuer or Freud to the patient that she should as far as possible communicate everything that came into her head, 'whether it was appropriate or not',[40] sounds like a trial formulation of the future *fundamental rule*.

However, the aspect in which the *Studies* come closest to the technique of psychoanalytic treatment is the exact observation and very advanced theoretical conceptualization of the phenomenon of *resistance*.[41] Freud was prepared early on to regard resistance not as something avoidable, disturbing and arbitrary but as a necessary and regular element, to be investigated and worked with. 'In the course of this difficult work,' he reports in the case history of Elisabeth von R., 'I began to attach a deeper significance to the resistance offered by the patient in the reproduction of her memories and to make a careful collection of the occasions on which it was particularly marked.'[42] This text already contains the archaeological metaphor of analytic work that had been spotted at once by the perspicacious early reviewer Alfred von Berger, where the 'procedure [...] of clearing away the pathogenic psychical material layer by layer' is compared with 'the technique of excavating a buried city'.[43]

Yet the impression conveyed of the process of *interpretation* is still somewhat one-dimensional. This is not principally because of its emphasis on the detective work of reconstruction, on exposure of the repressed link between trauma and symptom — that is to say, its disregard for the constructive, meaning–conferring aspects that have taken centre stage since Freud's late paper 'Constructions in analysis'.[44] Compared with classical psychoanalytic interpretation, the *Studies* lack not only the depth dimension of infantile impressions and wishes — i.e. of phantasies — but also dream analysis, although Freud does indicate in a footnote that he is already engaged on the investigation of his own dreams.[45] However, the

---

40 Ibid.: 154.
41 Cf., for example, ibid.: 268f.
42 Ibid.: 154.
43 Ibid.: 139.
44 Freud 1937d.
45 Freud 1895d: 69.

vital missing element is interpretation of the *transference*. It is fascinating to see, in the course of our reading, how this second key concept of genuinely psychoanalytic procedure literally begins to dawn on Freud – theoretically – in the very last pages of the book, albeit *after* the conclusion of his clinical work as described in the case reports. Even the idea of the *transference neurosis* seems to appear in a momentary flash. But years were in fact to pass before Freud succeeded in turning his discovery to full technical account – that is, in coming to see the transference as a process that structured the entire treatment and whose manifestations had to be interpreted unremittingly. Nevertheless, a plethora of intimations and indications of the transference can already be identified in the case histories of the *Studies*; even *countertransference* phenomena are reported, although, of course, without being recognized as such. But because the evidential force of the transference in the process of analytic understanding had not yet been understood, there was no need to assure its undisturbed development by strict neutrality on the part of the analyst and constancy of the therapeutic framework. These fundamental elements of fully fledged psychoanalytic technique, *abstinence* and the *setting*, will also be sought in vain in the *Studies*. Present-day psychoanalysts may also miss the aspect of considered *timing*. Interpretations are mostly given instantly, as soon as a hitherto unconscious connection is recognized – that is, without regard to the patient's capacity to assimilate them at any given time: 'She [Elisabeth von R.] cried aloud when I put the situation drily before her with the words: "So for a long time you had been in love with your brother-in-law."'[46]

Yet an observation made by Freud some thirty years after the book's publication and not long before Breuer's death is as true today as it was then: 'The cathartic method was the immediate precursor of psycho-analysis; and, in spite of every extension of experience and of every modification of theory, is still contained within it as its nucleus'.[47] Already in 1908, in a letter to C.G. Jung, he had not hesitated to describe the subject matter of the *Studies on Hysteria* as 'the first phase of our theory'.[48] Here are reasons enough to call this work the 'primal book of psychoanalysis'.

---

46 Ibid.: 157.
47 Freud 1924f: 194.
48 Freud 1974a [1906–13]: 159.

V

The fact that it took some time for the status of the book to be recognized was presumably an aftereffect of the alienation between the two authors. As can be reconstructed from the Fliess letters, the decision to publish their joint research was taken in summer 1892 while they were 'still in complete agreement'.[1] But about two years later, when the writing of the book was in its closing stages, Freud was already reporting that 'the scientific contact with Breuer has stopped'.[2] The differences between the two men's theoretical and technical conceptions cannot be discussed in detail here; the reader will in any case encounter the aetiological controversy – hypnoid hysteria versus defence hysteria – at every step. Freud's repeated subsequent allegation that Breuer was unwilling to accept his assessment of the importance of sexuality in the genesis of neurosis seems not to be borne out by the text of 'Theoretical'; but there do appear to have been disagreements, no doubt in fact on this point, during selection of the case material to be published.[3] Breuer himself later acknowledged in the letter to Auguste Forel quoted earlier that 'this immersion in the sexual in theory and practice is not to my taste', albeit after expressly emphasizing that the theme stemmed wholly from the 'largely very unexpected findings of medical experience' – that is, that it had empirical origins.[4]

The reader may discern a number of indirect expressions of distance and distancing in the text of the *Studies* itself, and in particular in the two concluding chapters, over whose composition the shadow of the authors' mutual alienation already loomed. Freud not only appears here as the independent discoverer of the transference, self-confidently referring again and again to the pressure procedure as 'my technique',[5] but also, so to speak writing himself away from Breuer and sketching out his future life-work, announces a broadening of his research interests beyond hysteria: 'Thus, starting out from Breuer's method, I found myself engaged in a consideration of the aetiology and mechanism of the neuroses *in general*.'[6] He now also forcefully stresses the involvement of the sexual factor in aetiology.

Near the closing section on the transference, he gives in the space of a few pages what is perhaps the most specific exposition of the psycho-analytic method we have from his pen. In it, he outlines the model of

---

1   Freud 1985c [1887–1904]: 32.
2   Ibid.: 86.
3   Ibid.: 74.
4   Ackerknecht 1957: 171 and 170.
5   Freud 1895d: e.g. 283.
6   Ibid.: 257 (my italics).

multidimensional organization, of the concentric stratified structure of the pathogenic psychic material; corrects the comparison with the 'foreign body' he had formerly arrived at with Breuer and replaces it by an analogy with an 'infiltrate';[7] and attempts to describe how, in the course of analytic work, one should move about in this memory archive that is ordered by a number of different principles of arrangement so as to 'get hold of a piece of the logical thread'.[8] The relevant passage, which also fascinated Alfred von Berger, is rich in imagery and contains the following comment, which Freud places in parentheses:

> (I am making use here of a number of similes, all of which have only a very limited resemblance to my subject and which, moreover, are incompatible with one another. I am aware that this is so, and I am in no danger of over-estimating their value. But my purpose in using them is to throw light from different directions on a highly complicated topic which has never yet been represented. I shall therefore venture to continue in the following pages to introduce similes in the same manner, though I know this is not free from objection.)[9]

This sounds like a reply to Breuer's warning, expressed a little earlier in his chapter on theory, about the danger 'of allowing ourselves to be tricked by our own figures of speech'.[10] Dissonances also emerge in the two men's assessment of their joint contribution to the investigation of hysteria. Whereas Freud was thoroughly imbued with the idea of having seen and formulated something for the very first time, Breuer, who in any case argues more explicitly than Freud from *within* the scientific context of the time, repeatedly quoting the relevant investigators of hysteria – especially Alfred Binet and Pierre Janet – concludes with this levelling and relativizing statement: '[...] so many excellent observers and acute minds have concerned themselves with hysteria. It is unlikely that any of their formulations was without a portion of the truth'.[11] However, it was precisely this attitude of cautious balancing, this unwillingness or inability to commit himself, that had irritated Freud about Breuer. In a letter to Fliess written just under a year after the book was published, Freud says: 'I believe he will never forgive that in the *Studies* I dragged him along and involved him in something where he unfailingly knows three candidates for the position of *one* truth and abhors all generalizations, regarding them as

---

7 Ibid.: 290.
8 Ibid.: 292.
9 Ibid.: 291.
10 Ibid.: 228.
11 Ibid.: 250.

presumptuous.'[12] Breuer would probably have found little to disagree with in this characterization of his scepticism, considering that he had once described himself to Fliess in the following terms: 'it is just that in all my opinions and actions, the thought occurs to me that everything might perhaps be quite different from the way I assume it to be'.[13]

The two men were indeed so irreconcilably antithetical in temperament that the alienation between them was unavoidable. Breuer did not share Freud's unconditionality, rigorism and willingness to take risks. Nor, presumably, did he possess the same genius and energy, as witness another letter from Breuer to Fliess written not long after the publication of the *Studies*: 'Freud's intellect is soaring at its highest. I gaze after him as a hen at a hawk'.[14] The gulf between them may have been exacerbated by the fact that Breuer, in displaying overwhelming generosity about the repayment of a debt, seems to have made Freud feel humiliated, thus in effect leaving him no choice but to show ingratitude,[15] and that Freud, who was suffering from worrying cardiac symptoms at the time of writing the *Studies*, was dissatisfied with Breuer as his doctor.

Let us in passing indulge in some highly speculative considerations about an obscure autobiographical note added by Freud to the case history of Miss Lucy R.,[16] the patient who knew and – because she did not 'want' to acknowledge it – at the same time did *not* know that she was in love with her employer. The footnote inserted by Freud at this point is quite puzzling to the general reader; it sounds as if he is addressing himself to a specific person who would surely know what he is talking about:

> [...]. I myself have had a very remarkable experience of this sort, which is still clearly before me. If I try to recollect what went on in my mind at the time I can get hold of very little. What happened was that I saw something which did not fit in at all with my expectation; yet I did not allow what I saw to disturb my fixed plan in the least, though the perception should have put a stop to it. I was unconscious of any contradiction in this; nor was I aware of my feelings of repulsion, which must nevertheless undoubtedly have been responsible for the perception producing no psychical effect. I was afflicted by that blindness of the seeing eye which is so astonishing in the attitude of mothers to their daughters, husbands to their wives and rulers to their favourites.

---

12 Freud 1985c [1887–1904]: 175.
13 Hirschmüller 1986: 256.
14 Jones 1953: 242.
15 Cf. Freud 1985c [1887–1904]: 294.
16 Freud 1895d: 117, n. 1.

Could it be that Freud was here attempting a delayed apology and explanation to Breuer for the incident many years before when he had rashly tried to free their gifted mutual friend Ernst Fleischl von Marxow, a patient of Breuer's, from his morphine addiction by means of cocaine, and had temporarily believed him to be cured, instead of recognizing the reality that Fleischl had now succumbed also to a cocaine addiction, which ultimately hastened his end? The comparisons adduced by Freud at the end of the footnote may indicate that he was groping his way towards the idea that, to use more modern terminology, such a 'blindness of the seeing eye' can arise when the perceiver perceives the other as a self-object distorted by his wishful thinking.

Be that as it may, the result of the alienation, which both Freud and Breuer experienced as painful, was that they in effect dropped their jointly written book immediately after it was published. Breuer turned his back on that entire field of research, while Freud withdrew cathexis from the book, quickly declared it to be obsolete in every respect and never again returned to many an important theme struck up in it for the first time; in particular, compared with his other works, he showed conspicuously little concern for its fate in terms of publishing. Having been out of print for a time, it did not appear in a new edition until 1909, and then, it seems, at the wish of Franz Deuticke, the publisher, rather than of Freud.[17] Each author wrote a separate short preface,[18] but neither made any revision to the text. The third and fourth editions, published in 1916 and 1922 respectively, were also unamended.

It was only when, in the mid-1920s, Freud included *Studies on Hysteria* in volume 1 of the *Gesammelte Schriften*, his first quasi-collected edition, that he manifestly began to own the work again.[19] He took possession of it in two ways: firstly, he omitted the two chapters composed by Breuer alone – after all, he could in any case not have put his name to texts which, unlike the 'Preliminary communication', he had not even co-authored – and, secondly, he added a number of footnotes to his own chapters and made a small number of textual amendments: for example, in the last sentence of the book he replaced the word 'Nervensystem' ['nervous system'] by 'Seelenleben' ['mental life']. From then on, the book was handed down for almost half a century so to speak as a *torso*, even in volume I of the *Gesammelte Werke*, the

---

17 Cf. Hirschmüller 1994: 20ff.
18 *SE* 2: xxxi.
19 It should, however, be mentioned that, with Breuer's consent, Freud had already had the 'Preliminary communication' reprinted in 1906 in the anthology *Sammlung kleiner Schriften zur Neurosenlehre aus den Jahren 1893–1906*, published under Freud's name (Leipzig and Vienna: Franz Deuticke: 14–29).

later compilation of collected works from the time of his exile. Freud was perfectly aware of its character as a torso. When C.G. Jung informed him in 1908 that Abraham A. Brill had suggested translating the *Studies* into English without Breuer's contributions, he had already objected: '[...] how can they put the book together without Breuer's "first case"? It is impossible and would be historically unjust. I should feel differently if Dr Brill wanted to translate the whole book.'[20] At any rate, with *Studies on Hysteria* appearing in the subsequent German editions as a torso, it henceforth became more difficult for readers to see it as the primal book of psychoanalysis: it is only by way of 'the book as a whole', as Virginia Woolf put it, that, in the second, distance-conferring phase of the reading process, we can arrive at a judgement and compare it with other books, whereas this is not yet possible in the first phase of receiving countless individual impressions: 'And the book as a whole is different from the book received currently in separate phrases.'[21] It is in fact only with the recent reprint of the first edition of a century ago that the *Studies* have become available again in their original language complete in one bound volume.[22]

All the same, throughout his life Freud struggled repeatedly with his intellectual debt of gratitude to Josef Breuer. There were reasons enough for this: what he had found useful was, after all, not only Breuer's initially greater experience of analytic work, nor merely the accelerating effect of their inspiring dialogue. A reading of 'Theoretical' suggests rather that it was mainly Breuer who encouraged Freud's interest in dreams, 'the normal hallucinatory state of healthy people'.[23] At any rate, this chapter already includes preliminary formulations of some of the laws of the dream-work – for example, that 'incompatible ideas can be present simultaneously without mutually inhibiting each other, as they do in waking life'.[24] In other words, the discussions with Breuer may have helped Freud so to

---

20 Freud 1974a [1906–13]: 120.
21 Woolf 1986 [1926]: 266f.
22 The two Breuer chapters were made accessible in the *Gesammelte Werke* again when the *Nachtragsband* [supplementary volume] was published in 1987.
23 Freud 1895d: 189.
24 Ibid.: 193. Being a well-read man, however, Breuer would surely have conceded that the subject of dreams was in people's minds given the contemporary climate of exploration of hypnotism and somnambulism. In his illuminating study, Gauld (1992) showed that, and explained why, the study of sleep, sleep-walking and dreams was already on the agenda in the early nineteenth century (cf., for instance, 114, 365, 399 and 540ff.). *A History of Hypnotism* in fact casts light on the well-prepared soil on which not only Breuer and Freud but also Bernheim, Charcot and Janet before them worked. That original spirit Azam, for example, had already reported on the detailed analysis of dreams, including his own, and advocated research in that field (1876b: 266f. and 269; 1877: 578f.).

speak to fix the position of the area of the mind whose scientific conquest he was then to describe in *The Interpretation of Dreams*,[25] the book with which he soon after came fully into his own. 'Theoretical' even contains a pointer towards *The Psychopathology of Everyday Life*.[26] Breuer ultimately appears in his texts as a man with a subtle gift for self-observation and the linguistic sensibility of an artist; one need only think of the passage in which – as if he already knew about the 'inner monologue', the 'stream of consciousness' – he describes how 'a stream of ideas and recollections runs through [a person's] consciousness [...] while his mind is at rest'.[27] During the many years of the two men's friendship, all this may well have helped to stimulate Freud's development into a writer.

And indeed, there are repeated references in Freud's later work to Breuer's contribution, some of them incidental and others featuring in the course of more detailed descriptions of that phase in the history of psychoanalysis. His assessment of the relationship between the cathartic method of treatment and psychoanalysis varies: as the quotations given above show, he usually stresses their continuity, while occasionally underlining the distance between them. Whereas the depiction of Anna O.'s therapy takes up so much space in the early *Five Lectures*[28] that Breuer appears almost as the father of psychoanalysis, Freud emphatically corrected this impression in his first 'official' historical account, 'On the history of the psycho-analytic movement'.[29]

Even though his indomitable striving for independence may sometimes have misled him into making public pronouncements in which the lines of provenance were severed, inside himself Freud seems to have kept the connection with Breuer alive. It is clear from the letters to Fliess how much he still respected Breuer's judgements after the end of their collaboration, even if they were usually now conveyed to him only secondhand. The case histories from the *Studies*, too, stayed with him. In an allusion to Alexandre Dumas, he wrote to C.G. Jung in 1909: 'In my university lectures, which I am now reorganizing as a seminar, [...] I have had two of the case histories from the *Studies* brought up to the level of our present knowledge (quinze

---

25 Freud 1900a.

26 Freud 1901b; cf. Freud 1895d: 222.

27 Freud 1895d: 205. Albeit principally in relation to hysterics, Janet had previously written the following about these patients' tendency to daydream: 'Toujours elles ont en tête une histoire interminable qui se déroule en spectacles visuels ou qui se raconte par la parole intérieure' ['They always have in their heads some interminable story that either unfolds in visual images or is narrated by the inner voice'] (n.d. [1894?]: 210). (On the 'stream of consciousness' in the context of Janet's work, cf. also Gauld 1992: 378ff. and 382f., n. 36.)

28 Freud 1910a.

29 Freud 1914d.

ans après)'.[30] And on a trip to the Rax mountain in 1928, he still recalled his conversation with Katharina.[31]

Very late in his life, in the traumatic circumstances of being a very sick old man under threat of death from Nazi persecution, Freud seems – despite the lack of relevant explicit indications in his work – to have returned once again to *Studies on Hysteria*, this time also on the theoretical level. Having for decades concentrated almost exclusively on the drive-related aspects of the genesis of neurosis and on the role of pathogenic phantasies, he now once more placed trauma in the foreground of his aetiological reflections – just as he had done in 'the past during his collaboration with Breuer.[32] A new upsurge of his self-analysis provided Freud for the first time with deep insights into archaic mechanisms of defence – in particular, *splitting*. This word may have formed the bridge that enabled him to turn back to the *Studies*, for splitting plays a central part in the primal book of psychoanalysis, even if the phrase 'splitting of the mind' used there means no more than the distinction, specific to hysteria, between ideas that are capable of entering consciousness and those that are not; in other words, it lacks the dimension of depth which Freud gave to the term in his very last texts, in the sense of a description of trauma-induced alterations of the ego, a dimension that was subsequently to impress its stamp on the modern psychoanalysis of not only narcissistic but also borderline and psychotic disturbances.

As if once more taking up and echoing the dialogue with Breuer, Freud, in his discussion of splitting in *An Outline of Psycho-Analysis*, published only after his death, writes that even in psychosis the ego is never altogether detached from reality: 'one learns from patients after their recovery that at the time in some corner of their mind (as they put it) there was a normal person hidden, who, like a detached spectator, watched the hubbub of illness go past him'.[33] Long before, Breuer had written the following about Anna O.'s two states of consciousness:

> Nevertheless, though her two states were thus sharply separated, not only did the secondary state intrude into the first one, but – and this was at all events frequently true, and even when she was in a very bad condition – a clear-sighted and calm observer sat, as she put it, in a corner of her brain and looked on at all the mad business.[34]

---

30 Freud 1974a [1906–13]: 266f. and n. 8.
31 Freud 1963a [1909–39]: 124.
32 Cf. Grubrich-Simitis 1988 [1987], and pp. 63f. below in the present book.
33 Freud 1940a [1938]: 202.
34 Freud 1895d: 46.

## VI

It is noteworthy that, when psychoanalysts began to concern themselves with the psychic sequelae of the Holocaust in first- and second-generation victims of persecution, they remembered *Studies on Hysteria*.[1] They were surely not conscious of the fact that Freud in his old age, in a premonition of the imminent Nazi crimes, had turned back to that early work of his in a similar way. They had at any rate noticed that, following the liberation of the first generation from the concentration camps, the symptoms often emerged only after a relatively long period of latency, and were thus reminded of the phenomenon of *Nachträglichkeit*[2] described in the *Studies*. In addition, the second generation displayed the same unusual combination of great intellectual and social prowess, on the one hand, and massive psychopathology, on the other, as had already astonished Breuer and Freud in the cases of Anna O., Emmy von N., Elisabeth von R. and Cäcilie M. in particular. Because of the temporarily clamorous symptoms exhibited precisely by second-generation patients – for example, the tendency to live in a double reality – these subjects were repeatedly diagnosed as suffering from schizophrenic psychosis, with drastic consequences for their therapeutic fate. The question therefore arose whether the term 'hysterical psychosis', used long before by Breuer and Freud in the *Studies*, might not be more suited to these acute but episodic hallucinatory irruptions.

At the 1973 International Psychoanalytical Congress in Paris – the very place where Freud had met Charcot – a re-evaluation of *Studies on Hysteria* had already been undertaken independently of the Holocaust research, in the context of a discussion about a modern psychoanalytic definition of hysteria. Connections had been forged with more recent research on outwardly inconspicuous, recurring traumatizations in the early mother–child relationship. The link between trauma and sexualization, so characteristic of the *Studies*, became relevant again.[3] Incidentally, the primal book of psychoanalysis even contains a preliminary formulation of the concept of 'cumulative trauma',[4] namely at the point where the authors note that, instead of a single, major trauma, 'a number of partial traumas forming a *group* of provoking causes [which] have only been able to exercise a traumatic effect by summation'[5] may be the crucial aetiological

---

1 Cf., in particular, Oliner 1982.
2 [*Translator's note*: The word *Nachträglichkeit* is usually translated elsewhere in the *Standard Edition* as 'deferred action', but this rendering is now controversial.]
3 For a summary, cf. Laplanche 1974.
4 Cf. Khan 1974 [1963]; cf. also Grubrich-Simitis 1981 [1979].
5 Freud 1895d: 6.

factor. In a word, the psychoanalysts confronted with the consequences of the Holocaust were able to take up these reflections from 1974, which allowed them to investigate the possibility of so to speak using Breuer's and Freud's early approach to hysteria to gain a better understanding of pathological mental states attributable to uniquely massive real traumatization and its transgenerational transmission.

These indications will surely suffice to demonstrate to the present-day reader that *Studies on Hysteria* is not merely of historical interest but also possesses modernity, even if this is not revealed at first glance. By attributing much more importance to traumatic factors in the causation of mental illness than was customary in the classical period from about 1900 until well into the second half of the twentieth century, when the focus was on drive aspects and phantasies, contemporary psychoanalysis has indeed reintegrated the substance of the book.


At the end of this commentary on the primal book of psychoanalysis, the work that flung wide open the door to the unconscious inner world of man a hundred years ago, let us turn for a moment to the general cultural scenery of the closing years of our own century, and enquire whether we should now be worrying that this door might gradually close again. In other words, might interest in the scientific investigation of subjective experiencing now be on the wane? At least two trends suggest that this might indeed be so: firstly, public attention nowadays is certainly focused on the spectacular progress of neurobiological research on mental phenomena – another reversal this, from mental life back to the nervous system – and secondly, in the field of psychotherapy, patients and therapists alike are proving increasingly unwilling to commit themselves to the sheer effort of long-term treatments at high frequency. The latter trend is just *one* of the numerous manifestations of the general tendency towards abbreviation and acceleration that permeates our society. However, Josef Breuer and Sigmund Freud were the first to understand that the unconscious internal world does not open up in fleeting, suggestion-based therapeutic contacts, and why this should be so. Against this background, a slow and painstaking reading of their *Studies on Hysteria* today would be a small act of resistance to the current of the times, and would persuade us of the aptness of Freud's simple sentence: 'Here, as elsewhere, a large change requires a large amount of work.'[6]

---

6   Ibid.: 278.

# Freud's Study of Moses as a Daydream:
## a biographical essay

### I

Freud was not an author who wrote material to be put away in a drawer. His writing was for publication. His constant concern that his works should remain accessible on the book market contrasted with his lack of interest in their preliminary stages. No sooner did he have the printed version in his hands than he threw away the handwritten papers from which it was made. It was not until 1914 that he became accustomed to preserve these documents, and then only because it had been pointed out to him that they might one day provide some pocket money for his grandchildren.[1] These manuscript sheets with their harmonious, weblike pattern of lines, as a rule virtually free of corrections, are of unusual beauty. Almost all of them are in fact fair copies – that is, in each case final versions.

It is therefore surprising, in the midst of such a classical landscape of manuscripts, to stumble across a jagged quarry. I refer to the part of the literary estate comprising the papers in Freud's hand for his last book, *Moses and Monotheism*,[2] which, in exile in London not long before his death, he had Allert de Lange publish in Amsterdam. One reason for my perusal of these manuscripts at the beginning of 1988 was that I was interested in the 'first version' described as long ago as 1941 by the editors of the *Gesammelte Werke*, in their foreword to the seventeenth volume, as a text that had been preserved and might possibly be 'put before the public at a later date'.[3] As we know from Freud's letters, the title of this version, which dates from 1934, was *Der Mann Moses: Ein historischer Roman* [The Man Moses: A

---

1  Cf. E. Freud, L. Freud and I. Grubrich-Simitis 1978 [1976]: 303.
2  Freud 1939a.
3  A. Freud, E. Bibring, W. Hoffer, E. Kris and O. Isakower 1941: ix.

Historical Novel]. I had long been fascinated by, in particular, the curious subtitle and wanted to investigate in what respects the early version differed from that published by Freud.[4]

At that time I presumed that the Moses manuscripts would conform to the model described above and comprise, on the one hand, the fair copy of the printed version and, on the other, the written text of precisely that early, rejected predecessor. They in fact turned out to contain both more and less than expected. As described in detail in the Appendix, all that survives of the three-part historical novel, apart from the plan of the contents, is the first part; of the three essays making up the printed version, the fair copies of only the second and third are preserved, while that of the first is missing. On the other hand, there is in addition a draft manuscript of a few passages from the third essay – the one which, according to Freud's own assessment, contains 'what was really objectionable and dangerous'.[5] These are preliminary formulations of those sections of the first part in which Freud draws an analogy between, on the one hand, his construction, in terms of the psychology and history of religion, of the genesis and effects of monotheism and, on the other, the aetiology of the neuroses – i.e. finds parallels between phenomena of group and individual psychology – and in which, in investigating the ultimate cause of the persuasive force and obsessional character of both religious ideas and pathogenic phantasies, he focuses on the concept of *trauma*.

The draft manuscript, whose very existence was, I believe, previously unknown, differs in a number of respects from the fair copy. What is more, it ends with five extra pages of notions recorded in telegraphic style for use in addenda, on which, however, Freud drew only for a few points that he incorporated in the published third Moses essay's second part, with which we are familiar.

As if in a soliloquy, he begins with the following resigned statement:[6] 'Too old and done too much scientific work to believe I have fully solved problem of religion. [I] know that here as elsewhere is only [a] contribution, [but] hopefully [an] important, hitherto lacking contribution.' Freud sometimes appears to depart from themes relevant to the study

---

4  I pursued this comparison further in my book *Back to Freud's Texts*, the original German version of which appeared *after* the present essay was first published (1996 [1993]: 199ff.).

5  Freud 1939a: 103 (translation slightly modified).

6  When reproducing extracts from the unpublished manuscripts, unless otherwise noted I have expanded abbreviations; I have done so tacitly where there was no ambiguity, and in angle brackets in other cases. Other additions of mine appear in square brackets. [*Translator's note*: This convention has been reproduced in the translation; some of the insertions in square brackets are mine.]

of Moses and, as it were, to indulge in free-floating reflections on future developments in psychoanalytic theory. He criticizes the 'one-sided preference' given to the 'so-called economic factors'. The 'more object ⟨-related⟩ drives' should not be forgotten, 'because [the] other person may be both, [namely] sexual object [and] enemy-helper'. A little later he writes: 'Drive discussion belongs together with critique of economic one-sidedness.' This discussion of the drives was plainly intended to culminate in a further revision of the classification of the drives.

The telegraphic-style notions also deal with the restriction of drives: 'Progressive drive restriction accompanies, indeed determines[, the] development of civilization.' For this reason civilization necessarily entails the 'temptation to regression'. The weakness of the repression corresponds to the degree of the prevailing renunciation. The 'healthiest' degree of drive restriction has 'not yet [been] found'. As an adherent of the nineteenth-century theory of evolution with its principle of passive adaptation, Freud wonders how it was possible for such 'inconsistencies' between drive-related wishes on the one hand and the exigencies of reality on the other to arise, because, after all, as he says, the psychic apparatus has developed phylogenetically by a process of adapting to the 'demands of reality'. His answer is that the reality that long ago compelled the evolution of the human species and gave rise to the organic substrate of the psyche no longer exists; however, the 'drives like everything organic are conservative [and] remain attuned to the earlier reality'. The 'organic [...] dies of its past'. Again, the 'organ⟨ic⟩ [is] by its nature prepared for self-destruction'.

I cannot go into more detail here about these succinct notations, which are manifestly of great present-day relevance.[7] The study and editing of the Moses manuscripts dating from the years 1934 to 1938, as well as their publication, are a task for the future; but however difficult, this task will also be a fascinating component of the project for a historical–critical edition of the *œuvre* in the original German. The question that had arisen in my mind when I first perused the manuscripts was as follows: why did the author not follow his usual custom of destroying these papers, except for the fair copy, once the book appeared in 1939? Considering the nature of the printed version, I also wondered why he published this text at all. For it exhibits the same fragmentary nature as that of the manuscripts and is a document of overstrain and partial failure – and moreover, uniquely in the Freudian canon, this is so in terms of both form and content.

Whereas Freud's textual compositions normally possess a harmonious structure as a matter of course, the printed version of his study of Moses

---

7   More information can be found in the Appendix, pp. 103ff.

comprises a string of three essays that differ in scale to a positively eccentric degree, the second being about four, and the third ten, times as long as the first. Unlike his other books, it has no preface of any kind. Instead, the third essay is introduced by two prefatory notes, one composed in Vienna 'Before March 1938' and the other in London in 'June 1938' – and not far from the end of the book is a summary that is actually a third proem. This peculiarity in the matter of prefaces is very likely a concomitant of the work's publication history: Freud had brought out the first and second essays in succession in his journal *Imago* while still in Vienna in 1937, so that only the third essay was being presented to the public for the first time in the book edition and may therefore have seemed to the author to require a separate introduction.[8]

For that reason, too, the third essay is the one that most insistently betrays the book's deficiencies of content. Repetitions make for circular argument. Passages in which the writer gives uninhibited rein to speculative flights of ideas and his delight in story-telling stand alongside coolly precise issue-taking with the views of scientific authors. Yet the latter element gives the impression more of a ritualized academic duty lacking in cogency, because, even when unable to refute expert views that conflict with his own, Freud is by no means prepared to abandon his pet theses, but instead decks them out all the more splendidly in suggestive chains of conclusions. His associations sometimes lead him to jump from subject to subject, and occasionally the thread seems to break.

Freud was extremely aware of these defects and it is not only in his letters that he mentions them again and again. In the book too, he emphasizes that his conclusions are based solely on *psychological* probabilities and lack *objective* evidence:

> Not even the most tempting probability is a protection against error; even if all the parts of a problem seem to fit together like the pieces of a jig-saw puzzle, one must reflect that what is probable is not necessarily the truth and that the truth is not always probable. And lastly, it did not seem attractive to find oneself classed with the schoolmen and Talmudists who delight in exhibiting their ingenuity without regard to how remote from reality their thesis may be.[9]

---

8 As described in more detail in the Appendix, the Moses manuscripts are accompanied by an outline of the contents which indicates that Freud, again in London, first considered *separate* publication of this third piece too, together with the two prefatory notes. He seems only later to have had the idea of including the two essays already published. Some of the formal idiosyncrasies may therefore conceivably be attributable to this decision, taken late in the process of preparation, to combine all three essays in the book.

9 Freud 1939a: 17.

Freud bluntly condemns the work's compositional disharmony as 'inartistic' and avers that he unreservedly deplores it.[10]

There must have been compelling reasons indeed for the fact that he nevertheless remained undeterred not only from writing down his reflections but also from eventually publishing them and preserving the preparatory manuscripts.

## II

Before turning to these reasons, let us briefly recall the main ideas put forward in Freud's study of Moses. The most telling summary of the work was provided by the author himself in a letter to Lou Andreas-Salomé, when he was still intending to withhold it from publication. The description runs as follows:[1]

> It started out from the question as to what has really created the particular character of the Jew, and came to the conclusion that the Jew is the creation of the man Moses. Who was this Moses and what did he bring about? The answer to this question was given in a kind of historical novel. Moses was not a Jew but a well-born Egyptian, a high official, a priest, perhaps a prince of the royal dynasty, and a zealous supporter of the monotheistic faith, which the Pharaoh Amenhotep IV had made the dominant religion round about 1350 BC. With the collapse of the new religion and the extinction of the eighteenth dynasty after the Pharaoh's death this ambitious and aspiring man had lost all his hopes and had decided to leave his fatherland and create a new nation which he proposed to bring up in the imposing religion of his master. He resorted to the Semitic tribe which had been dwelling in the land since the Hyksos period, placed himself at their head, led them out of bondage into freedom, gave them the spiritualized religion of Aten and as an expression of consecration as well as a means of setting them apart introduced circumcision, which was a native custom among the Egyptians and only among them. What the Jews later boasted of their

10 Ibid.: 103. In a passage from the fair copy of the third essay (manuscript page 52) that did not find its way into the printed version, Freud noted that the 'difficulties of the subject matter' had 'put his art of constructive portrayal to a test to which it had not [been] equal'. The sentence concerned fell victim to a revision of the textual structure when Freud, as again discussed more fully in the Appendix, decided to follow the first part of the third essay not merely with addenda but with a second part of its own.

1 Freud 1966a [1912–36]: 204f.

god Jahve, that he had made them his Chosen People and delivered them from Egypt, was literally true – of Moses. By this act of choice and the gift of the new religion he created the Jew.

Freud continues:

These Jews were as little able to tolerate the exacting faith of the religion of Aten as the Egyptians before them. A non-Jewish scholar, Sellin, has shown that Moses was probably killed a few decades later in a popular uprising and his teachings abandoned. It seems certain that the tribe which returned from Egypt later united with other kindred tribes which dwelt in the land of Midian (between Palestine and the west coast of Arabia) and which had adopted the worship of a volcano god living on Mount Sinai. This primitive god Jahve became the national god of the Jewish people. But the religion of Moses had not been extinguished. A dim memory of it and its founder had remained. Tradition fused the god of Moses with Jahve, ascribed to him the deliverance from Egypt and identified Moses with priests of Jahve from Midian, who had introduced the worship of this latter god into Israel.

In reality Moses had never heard the name of Jahve, and the Jews had never passed through the Red Sea, nor had they been at Sinai. Jahve had to pay dearly for having thus usurped the god of Moses. The older god was always at his back, and in the course of six to eight centuries Jahve had been changed into the likeness of the god of Moses. As a half-extinguished tradition the religion of Moses had finally triumphed. This process is typical of the way a religion is created and was only the repetition of an earlier process. Religions owe their compulsive power to the *return of the repressed*; they are reawakened memories of very ancient, forgotten, highly emotional episodes of human history. I have already said this in *Totem and Taboo*; I express it now in the formula: the strength of religion lies not in its *material*, but in its *historical* truth.

Lou Andreas-Salomé would immediately have understood that Freud is here alluding to his speculative theory of the murder of the primal father in the prehistoric family, a deed to which he had traced back the genesis of totemism, the taboo on incest and the sense of guilt – in a word, the beginnings of civilization. Put differently, Freud is saying that the monotheistic religions – and he includes Christianity in his reflections – have such a powerful impact not because their assertions are true but because their traditions preserve in memory that prehistoric tragedy, albeit in distorted form.

In the final paragraph of the letter, Freud puts forward some external and internal considerations that are of the greatest importance for an understanding of his study of Moses:

And now you see, Lou, this formula, which holds so great a fascination for me, cannot be publicly expressed in Austria today, without bringing down upon us a state prohibition of analysis on the part of the ruling Catholic authority. And it is only this Catholicism that protects us from the Nazis.[2] And furthermore the historical foundations of the Moses story are not solid enough to serve as a basis for these invaluable conclusions of mine. And so I remain silent. It suffices me that I myself can believe in the solution of the problem. It has pursued me throughout the whole of my life.

Forgive me, and with cordial greetings from your

Freud

This account, which dates from 6 January 1935, must be supplemented with some further information for the purposes of my argument. The external threat increased to an extreme pitch in the ensuing years of work on the Moses manuscripts. As a man with an indomitable aspiration to independence, Freud had, over the decades, created a life-work of worldwide significance, and had founded a science of his own, a scientific organization of his own and a publishing house of his own. All this threatened to be smashed under the Nazi persecution, and it was indeed smashed. His books having already been burned in 1933, the psycho-analytic research and training institutions were dissolved one after another and finally the publishing house too was wound up. However, it was only when his children were interrogated by the Gestapo in 1938 that Freud's disavowal of the immediate danger to his life weakened sufficiently for him to be prepared to emigrate. His external fate of persecution, with the experience of being impotently at the mercy of events, was rendered even more acute by an internal persecutory situation. Freud was not suffering just from the restrictions of advanced age; for years a cancer had been attempting, as he once put it, to take his place.[3] He was therefore faced with a total threat not only to his life-work but also, literally, to his life.

Nor is it clear from Freud's letter to Lou Andreas-Salomé, which outlines the main ideas of the 'historical novel', that the more complex printed version does not admit of a reading solely in terms of the history

---

2   Freud corrected this error in June 1938 in his 'Prefatory Note II' to the printed version: 'Catholicism proved, to use the words of the Bible, "a broken reed"' (1939a: 57).
3   Cf. Schur 1972: 520.

and psychology of religion. Passages of the book are nothing other than a formulation of the principles of psychoanalysis and an obvious exemplification of its method. Other parts of the text, in a kind of retrospective theorization, open up sudden vistas through the various strata in the formation of Freud's theoretical edifice, from the late stages back to the early ones – for example, from the drive theory to the trauma theory of the aetiology of the neuroses. In some cases, new and old terminology are abruptly juxtaposed. Sentences in which dogmatic tendencies appear to prevail are succeeded by reflections that display a fresh agile-mindedness brimming with life wherein the author raises questions to which he does not yet have answers. Freud repeatedly maintained that the study of Moses had been occasioned by the then raging hurricane of anti-Semitism: he wanted to know how it had come about that the Jews had 'attracted this undying hatred'.[4] Seen in these terms, the book was at the time also a kind of polemic. Finally, as will be shown below, it can be regarded as a continuation of Freud's concealed autobiographical communications. At any rate, it is many things all at once: psychology of religion; biblical criticism; fictional rewriting of a myth; a history of the formation of Freudian theory; a monograph on the genesis of individual and collective neurosis; a recapitulation of the theory of civilization; psychohistory; a political treatise; and a metaphorical autobiography.

Freud had no doubt originally intended to signal the eccentric position of *Moses and Monotheism* in the strict canon of the œuvre by the subtitle 'A Historical Novel'.[5] Some readers who are not at all ill-disposed towards psychoanalysis even now react with irritation to the book. In my view, a closer approach is possible to the specific off-putting character of the study of Moses if the work is read as a kind of *daydream* generated under traumatic conditions of extreme distress. This does not on any account mean that other lines of research on Freud's last book – for instance, through the disciplines of religious science, social psychology, ancient history, evolutionary biology or the history of language – cannot be equally

---

4   Freud 1968a [1927–39]: 91.
5   Another reason for Freud's choice of this genre attribution may be that he was replying to Eduard Meyer, some of the conclusions of whose book *Die Israeliten und ihre Nachbarstämme*, published in 1906, he disputes in *Moses and Monotheism*. On the question of Moses as a historical figure, Meyer had commented dismissively that it was 'not the task of historical research to invent novels'. This quotation was recently taken up by Rudolf Smend (1995: 20), who described how, over the course of time, Moses had ultimately been reduced by 'four big subtractions' to a mere figure of legend. However, he also showed how a modern biblical scholar can, by taking certain recurring subjects seriously – that is, in an approach perfectly analogous to Freud's – still deem it possible for Moses to have been a historical personage.

legitimate and illuminating. In the following I deliberately confine myself to just *one* of the work's many planes of meaning with a view to understanding the peculiarities of the Moses manuscript and printed text described above, which I take to be tokens of a daydream structure.

As an investigator, Freud of course devoted a great deal of attention to daydreams. He had already noted in *The Interpretation of Dreams*:

> Like dreams, they are wish-fulfilments; like dreams, they are based to a great extent on impressions of infantile experiences; like dreams they benefit by a certain degree of relaxation of censorship. If we examine their structure, we shall perceive the way in which the wishful purpose that is at work in their production has mixed up the material of which they are built, has rearranged it and has formed it into a new whole.[6]

In daydreams, too, the typical mechanisms of the dream-work – condensation, displacement and considerations of representability – are stated to be operational. Freud also stressed that the hero of the daydream is always the phantasying subject himself, 'either directly or by an obvious identification with someone else'.[7] Finally, he emphasized the particular relationship between the daydream and the structure of time, noting that the daydream hovered between 'the three moments of time which our ideation involves',[8] in so far as the motivating wish 'makes use of an occasion in the present to construct, on the pattern of the past, a picture of the future'.[9]

For his own daydream, Freud in 1934 chose a subject whose contours have become blurred by the obscurity of ancient history and which therefore lends itself particularly well to refashioning in accordance with the purposes of the wish. His main concern in his last book, no doubt, was indeed to fulfil a wish in phantasy: to allay the grinding disquietude he felt about the future of his life-work. I conjecture that the threat posed by the Nazi terror was thus the 'occasion in the present' which gave rise to that extensive daydreaming in the almost eighty-year-old Freud. Using material from the past – the reading of the Torah that was familiar to him from his childhood – Freud sought to sketch out a confidence-inspiring image of the future: by the example of the fate of the man Moses and of monotheism, he demonstrated to himself how an uncomfortable, demanding doctrine does not perish even when politically persecuted and suppressed, but, on the

---

6  Freud 1900a: 492.
7  Freud 1916–17a: 99.
8  Freud 1908e: 147.
9  Ibid.: 148.

contrary, returns from repression after a long interval, and relies precisely on this diphasic character for the development of its full effectuality. My thesis seems to be borne out by the fact that, in the Moses study, Freud at one point compares the 'delayed effect'[10] of a *scientific* doctrine to the latency period of monotheism. His example is Darwin's theory of evolution, which likewise 'awoke emotional resistances'[11] and, as he says, gained acceptance only by a discontinuous process that took a considerable length of time. As we know, Freud had stressed elsewhere the parallel between his psychoanalysis and Darwinism.[12]

An exhaustive interpretation of such a condensed, overdetermined entity as the Moses study is, of course, not possible, and not only because a number of wishes have found expression in it. Even if we take account of Freud's letters and thematically related works, and include in our examination also the unpublished passages of the Moses manuscripts as, so to speak, additional associations, we cannot even approach the level of certainty attainable at best in analytic dialogue. From this point of view, any attempt to interpret suppressed, preconscious and unconscious elements of a text without the possibility of comment by its author is bound to suffer from a degree of inadequacy and indeed impermissibility. However, since the peculiarities of the manuscript and printed text of Moses cannot be understood in terms solely of the manifest, I should like to make two attempts at interpretation.

If the central purpose that gave rise to the daydream had to do with the survival of psychoanalysis – following Freud's classification, this would be a matter of an ambitious wishful dynamic serving 'to elevate the subject's personality'[13] – it is possible to distinguish within it, as it were descending from the surface of consciousness, two tendencies: first, the wish to close gaps in the edifice of his own doctrine, in the process reconceptualizing the characteristic features of psychoanalysis that make it emotionally so uncomfortable; and second, the wish, through the identification with the man Moses and the impact he had, to make certain of his own immortality, while at the same time holding in check a regressive internal process by which Freud, under the pressure of persecution, perhaps felt threatened.

---

10 Freud 1939a: 66.
11 Ibid.: 67.
12 For example, 1917a: 140f.
13 Freud 1908e: 147.

### III

Let us begin with the first wish. It is no coincidence that Freud, under the influence of precisely these traumatic life circumstances, now returns to the role of *trauma* in the formation of neurotic and psychotic symptoms. The study of Moses is his last attempt to link the trauma and drive models of the aetiology of the neuroses – that is, his preanalytic theory and his psychoanalytic theory proper of the causation of psychopathology.

The following rough outline may be given of this complex subject matter.[1] The preanalytic trauma model places the aetiological focus on an overwhelming *external* event – a sexual act or scene to which the patient was exposed in childhood and which has its harmful effect on a *deferred* basis by way of a subsequent process of repression; the pathogenesis is therefore diphasic. However, Freud came to realize from his careful clinical work that his patients' reports of such seductions did not always correspond to actual events, but reproduced recurring phantasy configurations. In his step-by-step investigation of these entities, Freud was then led to the discovery of the unconscious *internal world* of man, of infantile sexuality as epitomized in the drive model, of the various phases of libidinal development corresponding to the relevant erogenic zones of the body, and of the structure of the Oedipus complex. Whereas the more conventional trauma model applied to the *pathogenesis* of the comparatively small number of people who had been sexually violated in childhood, the revolutionary drive model is concerned with the *psychogenesis* of everyone.

Freud knew that the outrage provoked by his discovery of the unflattering internal world would not abate and would therefore again and again give rise to the need to reconsign everything to oblivion. For this reason he constantly emphasized the *internal* factors in his aetiological theory. Contrary to the simplistic assertions of some critics who all too readily find a hearing nowadays, it would surely never have occurred to him to underestimate the significance of external reality in the causation of psychic illness. This can be demonstrated by many passages, for the most part admittedly inconspicuous, in his *œuvre* and not, therefore, only in the works on the theory of civilization and in the explicit discussions of the traumatic neuroses. Towards the end of his life, now that he himself was under the distressing pressure of a traumatic political reality, he perhaps felt a need, in his study of Moses, to restore the *external* aetiological factors to

---

1  I discussed this subject more fully in 'Trauma or drive – drive and trauma' (Grubrich-Simitis 1988 [1987]).

the foreground of his theorization, in order to fill what might upon a superficial examination appear to be a gap in his teaching.

In the passage in the third essay where Freud is seeking an analogy in individual psychology to help explain the genesis and effect of the mono-theistic idea, he adopts an approach at variance with the early seduction theory and includes among the aetiological traumas not only massive 'impressions of a sexual and aggressive nature' – i.e. overwhelming experiences – but also 'early injuries to the ego (narcissistic mortifications)'.[2] The central pathogenic factor might even be 'only an early emotional relationship',[3] whose adverse eventual consequences include permanent alterations of the ego, mediated, as we would now add, by processes of projective identification.[4] These formulations are at any rate perfectly consistent with more modern psychoanalytic theories of the traumatic genesis of the narcissistic and perverse, borderline and psychotic disturbances.

Soon, however, Freud in his Moses study breaks off this clinically well-founded discussion of trauma and its effects in the early stages of ontogenesis and returns to the phylogenetic speculation on the murder of the primal father and the origins of totemism, commenced in *Totem and Taboo*[5] and continued in the draft of the twelfth metapsychological paper,[6] a speculation initially inspired in him by the animal phobias of children. There he had attempted to imagine the real traumatic events in the life of the early human horde – driving out, castration and murder – which in his view might possibly be handed down as an 'archaic heritage' in the unconscious phantasies of those living today.

Considered in these terms, the phylogenetic speculation does indeed constitute a bridge between the trauma and drive models. At the same time Freud was providing himself with an answer to one of the main questions raised by his study, namely that of the origin of the powerful effect of monotheism. His conclusion was that the power of the two great monotheistic religions – Christianity as well as Judaism – was so compelling because in them the primaeval tragedy returned from repression, albeit in distorted form, while at the same time the primal father, in the form of the *one* god, was restored to his rights.

---

2  Freud 1939a: 74.
3  Ibid.: 75.
4  Freud is thus here applying to pathogenesis an earlier general finding concerning the formation of the ego, and de facto laying the foundations of the theory of object relations: 'At the very beginning, in the individual's primitive oral phase, object-cathexis and identification are no doubt indistinguishable from each other.' The character of the ego 'is a precipitate of abandoned object-cathexes' (1923b: 29).
5  Freud 1912–13a.
6  Freud 1985a [1915].

It is noteworthy that Freud makes no mention of the quite different, less far-fetched and much more obvious explanation of the powerful impact of religious ideas that he had previously postulated in *The Psychopathology of Everyday Life*:

> In point of fact I believe that a large part of the mythological view of the world, which extends a long way into the most modern religions, *is nothing but psychology projected into the external world.* The obscure recognition (the endopsychic perception, as it were) of psychical factors and relations in the unconscious is mirrored [...] in the construction of a *supernatural reality,* which is destined to be changed back once more by science into the *psychology of the unconscious.*[7]

In 1927 – that is, not long before Freud began his reflections on Moses – Romain Rolland, after reading *The Future of an Illusion*,[8] critically pointed out to him that he had failed to acknowledge the true source of religious energy, namely the 'oceanic' feeling. Freud, with visible reluctance, took up the point in *Civilization and its Discontents* and mentioned this spontaneous 'feeling of an indissoluble bond, of being one with the external world as a whole',[9] which he related to the infant's modalities of perceiving and feeling *before* the establishment of subject–object differentiation – that is, prior to the setting up of articulated boundaries of the self that separate inside from outside. However, he did not accept that the oceanic feeling was the source of religious faith, which he instead ascribed to the universal helplessness of human beings during childhood and to a correspondingly pressing, but structured, longing for the father. In the discussion of the psychology of religion included in the study of Moses, possible contributions from the preverbal modes of ego functioning of ontogenesis are not mentioned at all. Even the one sentence that appears to point in this direction – 'A child's emotional impulses are intensely and inexhaustibly deep to a degree quite other than those of an adult; only religious ecstasy can bring them back'[10] – manifestly relates to the father dimension.

At this point a short biographical digression is called for. There is some evidence that Freud preferred to avoid delving into the phenomena of the very earliest stages of mental structuring – that is, of the primary mother

7 Freud 1901b: 258f.
8 Freud 1927c.
9 Freud 1930a [1929]: 65.
10 Freud 1939a: 134.

dimension. This was not only for practical reasons connected with his working economy or on account of his scepticism about the depth of field of the instrumentarium of psychoanalysis at the time, but no doubt also because he found the confrontation with this archaic sphere too threatening for him personally. He expressly emphasized that he found it difficult 'to work with these almost intangible quantities'.[11] A number of recent contributions indicate that Freud's own early experiences may not have been as unclouded as was long assumed by idealizing biographers.[12]

In retrospect, 'the happy child from Freiberg' presented to us by Freud in his letter to the Mayor of Příbor[13] in 1931 seems to have remained unquestioned by researchers for decades. The death of his brother Julius in infancy, when Freud was not yet two years old – that is, before the stabilization of the boundaries between self and object – has indeed hitherto, in accordance with the explanation advanced by Freud himself, been discussed primarily in terms of sibling rivalry: the fulfilment of the elder brother's wishes to get rid of the younger one is deemed to have left a precipitate of guilt feelings in the first-born. However, attention is seldom paid to the effects of this sudden event on the young mother, who was then pregnant with her third child and had lost a brother with the same forename just before the death of her son.[14] Yet we may surely think it probable that this twofold mourning-work abruptly modified, at

---

11 Freud 1930a [1929]: 72.

12 On the situation of external hardship in which Freud as a child and his family lived, cf., for example, the research of Josef Sajner (1968, 1981, 1988); see Harry T. Hardin (1987, 1988) for a summary review of various authors' studies of conjectured traumatizations suffered by Freud during those years.

13 Cf. Freud 1960a [1873–1939]: 406.

14 Cf. a genealogy of the Nathansohn family in the Sigmund Freud Collection at the Library of Congress, to which my attention was drawn by Harold P. Blum and which is said to have been made around 1930. It shows that Freud's mother was the only girl and that she had four brothers (Julius, Adolf, Nathan and Hermann). Julius is recorded as having been born in 1838, so that he was some three years younger than Amalia. The year of his death appears as '1857'. It was clearly not possible to determine the years of birth of the other brothers. For one of them only, Adolf, the year of death is noted: '1862'; he is stated to have been an 'advocate in Lemberg' when he died – also therefore fairly young. Nevertheless, he was probably older than Julius. The age order of the siblings in his mother's family seems not to have been clear even to Freud. In a 'Heredity questionnaire' (this English-language document, also in the Sigmund Freud Collection, presumably dates from 1925, because Freud quotes his mother's age as '90 years'), he simply wrote '?' in answer to a question about his mother's position in the birth order of her family of origin, whereas he knew that there were a total of '5' siblings. Completing the sentence 'You were the — child in a family of —', Freud filled in the first blank with '1' and the second with '7 (8)'; his own brother Julius, who died in infancy, was included in the count in parentheses.

least temporarily, the quality of the mother's availability to her eldest child.[15]

From this point of view, the 'happy child from Freiberg' is the child in its first year of life and at the beginning of its second, held in a deeply satisfying mother–child dyad that laid the foundations on which Freud was able to erect his gigantic *opus*. However, Freud's retrospective account of the time when he 'was about three', when 'the branch of industry in which my father was concerned met with a catastrophe', after which the family was forced to move from the country to a large town with the consequence of long 'and difficult years'[16] of helpless poverty,[17] is perhaps a displacement. It may be seen as an attempt to defend against the catastrophe of those early deaths in his second year of life, at an age of even greater susceptibility to irritation, and of their effects, so to speak, in the mother's branch of industry. Put differently, the relocation from Freiberg to Vienna, coupled with the associated loss of the extended family, had reactivated that catastrophic other experience in the child, capable as he now was of language and memory, although Freud was unable to recognize that something from an earlier time was being reactivated. At any rate, the trauma of object alteration and object replacement may be presumed to have resulted, in Freud's psyche, not only in that permeability of ego boundaries that is the precondition for creativity, but also in the enormous lifelong internal tension that drove him to deploy fully his innate genius and to take upon himself the consuming toil of bringing forth his life-work. The fact that, in his enormous efforts at self-analysis, he must have met with impenetrable resistances on this primary level of early traumatization is another matter; in any case, again and again he soberly stressed the limits of what could be achieved by self-analysis – and was still doing so during the gestation of the study of Moses.[18]

There is, of course, no evidence for this reconstruction of Freud's psychic beginnings. Latent remote effects of the early misfortune can be detected at best in reverberations in his texts, even if there is no mention in the manifestly autobiographical statements of distressing experiences affecting the structuring of his psyche. The Moses book proves to be a

15 In the contribution cited, H.T. Hardin postulates that the Catholic Czech nanny had at this time assumed the significance of a substitute mother and that the early alienation between the little Freud and his natural mother had subsequently been impossible to overcome. Consequently, the sudden disappearance of this nanny in the third year of Freud's life is deemed by this author to have been tantamount to yet another traumatic object loss, which Freud had to disavow throughout his life.

16 Freud 1899a: 312.

17 Cf. Freud 1985c: 374 (letter to Wilhelm Fliess of 21 September 1899).

18 Cf. Freud 1935b: 234.

text that bears the hallmarks of the re-experiencing in the present of that early injury.

Fainter vibrations may be sensed in other writings, and presumably also in certain theoretical pieces nowadays felt to be unsatisfactory. This applies, for example, to Freud's psychology of women, but also to some aspects of the phylogenetic speculation on catastrophes and crimes in the primaeval period. Interpreted along these lines, they could be seen as an attempt to come to terms with the consequences of his own ontogenetic pregenital traumatization through displacement into the prehistory of the species. After all, Freud referred to the first three years of human life as 'the prehistoric epoch'[19] and likened the relevant ego feeling, when it makes its presence felt in adulthood, to the crocodile, a representative of the 'race of great saurians'.[20] Again, at the time of the Moses study he could still write: 'One feels inclined to doubt sometimes whether the dragons of primaeval days are really extinct'[21] – from this point of view, the 'dragons of primaeval days' would be the consequences of catastrophic events of Freud's own early infancy that were still active within him.

Finally, it may be wondered whether Freud would have been able to endure so steadfastly the social isolation into which he was plunged as a result of the scandalous radicalism of his findings had this not fitted in with his own inherent tendency to stay on his own. After all, we know that dependence remained anathema to him throughout his life, and that his unconditional aim was independence on every level – not only in his own analysis and the provenance of his scientific ideas, but also from the classical university faculties and academic institutions and from established publishing houses. We may speculate that this may have been connected, too, with a compelling unconscious need to protect himself from experiences of loss and disappointment – that is to say, to avoid at all costs catastrophic feelings of getting lost, starving and being torn apart like those of his infancy.

This reconstructive digression, which is indispensable to the interpretation given below of the second wish discernible in the daydream, here forms the background to my conjecture that, in Freud's internal world, now that he was old and seriously ill, the terror of the Nazi persecution aroused echoes of that traumatization of infancy, so that, not least for this reason, he sought refuge in the phylogenetic construction when attempting, in his book on Moses, to explain the powerful effect of monotheistic religion.

---

19 Freud 1900a: 245.
20 Freud 1930a [1929]: 68.
21 Freud 1937c: 229.

After all, this construction allowed him to move in the sphere of narrative differentiation that is proper to the secondary process – so to speak, in that of the father dimension – instead of having to concern himself with the diffuse area of preverbality, which he may then have felt to be particularly threatening – that is, the early mother dimension. Considered in these terms, the advantage of the phylogenetic construction at the time was a subjective one. Its objective disadvantage today is that it is scientifically untenable in this form,[22] in particular owing to its reductionist assumptions about the life-styles of early man and because it takes unreservedly for granted the existence of a Lamarckian mode of hereditary transmission.[23] As to his postulated mechanisms for the passing on of memory traces of the archaic heritage, Freud presumably had doubts of his own, which seem to have found expression in a slip in the draft manuscript of the third essay, in which he wrote[24] that 'this state of affairs [was] not strictly proven', but 'that we can in any case [*ohnehin*]' – instead of 'without it [*ohne ihn*]' – 'not explain anything in group psychology'.

On this basis, Freud's wish that contributed to the formation of the daydream of the Moses study – to fill gaps in his work and to unite the trauma and drive models – is expressed directly in the *manifest* text. Conversely, the emphasis on specific features of psychoanalysis is implicit and can be inferred only as a *latent* message from certain conspicuous recurring characterizations in Freud's description of monotheism.

Again and again he refers to its *harshness*. It is stated to be harsh in the way it distinguishes itself from the traditions that prevailed until the time of its appearance. For example, Mosaic monotheism categorically rejects the disavowal of the finitude of human life that had stood at the centre of the traditional Egyptian religion; interpreting, we may add that psychoanalysis around the turn of the century adopted a similarly radical position in its demolition of the denial of adult, and in particular infantile, sexuality and in its systematic demonstration of the absurdity of the two fundamental convictions that mental life consisted essentially of consciousness and that there was a clear boundary between psychic normality and pathology. Monotheism is also harsh in its attitude to man's need for illusion. In its

---

22 This admittedly does not dispose of the fundamental questions raised by Freud in the study of Moses. For example, how are we to understand and indeed explain the undeniable phenomenon of the return of the repressed in accordance with certain rhythms, or the silent – that is, not manifestly verbal – transmission of traumatizations from one generation to the next? These are questions of the greatest importance not only clinically but also collectively, and psychoanalysts are still searching for answers to them today.

23 On this point, cf. Grubrich-Simitis 1987 [1985].

24 Manuscript page 18.

high valuation of the ethical, it rejects every form of magic and sorcery; and psychoanalysis, with its commitment to truth, likewise insists on a rational theory of the irrational and on a rational therapeutic technique, dispensing with suggestion and with promises that cannot be kept and demanding laborious and prolonged collaboration from the analysand. Finally, monotheism is harsh on the human craving for visual expression. By its ban on images – that is, the exclusion of seeing – Mosaic monotheism enforced a higher development of intellectuality and directed the gaze inwards; and one of the consequences of this withdrawal of attention from the periphery of perception – in effect a shift from sensory stimuli to those of the drives – was the discovery of the mind, which opened up the invisible field that is the province of psychoanalysis.

Even where Freud does not refer directly to his own demanding doctrine, he is nevertheless indirectly canvassing for it, by demonstrating the beauty of the psychoanalytic method and the attraction of its approach to texts. He reads the biblical records in the same way as one would interpret a dream or a parapraxis, adopting roughly the following rules: one should allow oneself to be guided by the meaning of the words; take 'noticeable gaps, disturbing repetitions and obvious contradictions' seriously and regard them as 'indications which reveal things to us which it [the text] was not intended to communicate';[25] and, finally, remain prepared to draw one's own conclusions spontaneously – like the clever Jewish boy in the joke who, when asked who the mother of Moses was, replied without hesitation: the Princess. '"No," he was told, "she only took him out of the water." "That's what *she* says," he replied, and so proved that he had found the correct interpretation of the myth.'

## IV

The joke quoted above appears not in the study of Moses but in the *Introductory Lectures on Psycho-Analysis*.[1] Freud must therefore already have been convinced some twenty years earlier of the validity of one of the main theses of his book.[2] What is certain is that the figure of Moses played a part

---

25 Freud 1939a: 43.

---

1 Freud 1916–17a: 161.
2 Indeed, the trail can be traced back even further – via a similar remark in 'A special type of choice of object made by men' (Freud 1910h: 174) to a discussion contribution of Freud's dating from 25 November 1908, on a paper by Otto Rank about the myth of the birth of the hero, which contains ideas that quite astonishingly anticipate those of the

in the moulding of his ego-ideal from the beginning. That brings me to the second wish that may have contributed to the shaping of this daydream. As we know, there is a long series of mythological and historical personages with whom Freud identified in succession or simultaneously, in both his waking and his dream life; this phenomenon was by no means confined to the structuring phase of his personality but continued into old age and had the function of constant self-correction and self-enrichment through tradition recalled, in the form of an imaginative and not uncommonly ironic pursuit of traces. Apart from Joseph, the central *biblical* identificatory figure of the unbeliever's later life was surely Moses.[3] The Moses representation surely belonged to the very core of Freud's self.

It not only becomes manifest in the two explicit writings – the essay 'The Moses of Michelangelo'[4] and the book *Moses and Monotheism* – but also appears again and again, directly or indirectly, in other works of Freud and in his letters. An example of its indirect occurrence is the passage in *The Interpretation of Dreams* where he describes one of his dreams of Rome, in which, from the top of a hill, he saw the city 'half-shrouded in mist [...] so far away', and observed in it the 'theme of "the promised land seen from afar"';[5] another is in a letter written during the First World War: '[...] I often feel as alone as during the first ten years when I was surrounded by a desert.'[6]

The Moses representation was used intrapsychically in a variety of ways and, as will now be shown, performed indispensable stabilizing functions. To argue along the traditional lines of Freud biography, one might begin by assuming that, in the Moses representation, Freud created for himself a father-figure with the qualities of a protector, leader and hero as a compensation for the anything but go-getting character of his real father. However, this would be to underestimate the importance of that real father, one of Freud's debts to whom was after all his familiarity with the tradition of the scriptures, whereby he was guided towards the figure of Moses, the

---

Moses study (Nunberg and Federn 1967: 63). Finally, it is conceivable that one of the deepest roots of Freud's conviction lies in his boyhood reading of the eleventh of Heinrich Heine's 'Zeitgedichte'; at any rate, he himself quotes the relevant line in his book on Moses (1939a: 30f., n. 2). For further possible sources of the hypothesis of Moses as an Egyptian, and, in particular, references to a text in Josef Popper-Lynkeus's *Phantasien eines Realisten* (1899), cf. Freud's letters to Yisrael Doryon of 7 and 25 October 1938 (Freud 1945–46a: 786ff.). Cf. also p. 77 below.

3  This is a common theme in the secondary literature on Freud; cf. recent contributions such as those of Robert (1976 [1974]), Bergmann (1976), Klein (1985), McGrath (1986) and Blum (1991).
4  Freud 1914b.
5  Freud 1900a: 194.
6  Freud 1966a [1912–36]: 32.

exemplar of the autonomous 'great man', as it were *born an adult*, whose childhood[7] and the dangers that threatened it are in fact hardly mentioned in the Bible.[8] Freud's own identification with this figure helped him defend against anxieties connected with helpless dependence and with the tug of regressive wishes – for such wishes would surely have put him in touch with the aftereffects of the traumatic experiences of loss and discontinuity during his own infancy. From this point of view, the Exodus may have appeared to Freud as an allegory of an individuation that does eventually prove successful, and the lure of the Egyptian fleshpots as a metaphor of the dangers of detachment from symbiosis. In addition, the biblical hero, described as energetic, ambitious and irascible, may have served Freud, especially in his youth, as a sublimation model; for his career proved in effect that even such a passionate person may succeed in – to use the wording of the Moses study's chapter headings – achieving 'drive renunciation', making an 'advance in intellectuality' and creating an intellectual life-work. Last but not least, the identification with Moses helped to consolidate Freud's Jewish identity; he was convinced that the Jews had derived their unparalleled staying power over the millennia from the Mosaic tradition.

At times of severe stress, Freud's identification with Moses seems to have expanded and penetrated into consciousness, with simultaneous strengthening and threatening effects. The Nazi persecution was not the first occasion when this occurred; it had already happened in the period of the conflict and eventual break with C.G. Jung, whom Freud had, of course, seen for a while as the continuator of his work, as the following sentence taken from a letter written in 1909 shows: '[...] if I am Moses, then you are Joshua and will take possession of the promised land of psychiatry, which I shall only be able to glimpse from afar.'[9] A few years later, it was plainly no longer possible to overlook the fact that Jung had abandoned the concept of infantile sexuality and returned to a therapeutic technique thought to be obsolete. Freud apparently saw the inevitable public polemic with his former adherent as the first truly serious threat to psychoanalysis.[10]

---

7 If we give credence to Harry T. Hardin's thesis reproduced on p. 67, n. 15, even the identification with the child Moses might have been attractive to Freud when he read the Torah as a boy: although the baby Moses is exposed by his own mother, albeit in order to save his life, and is rescued from the water by the princess, a traumatic change of object does not occur because Moses' sister manages to get the princess to engage the foundling's natural mother as his nurse, so that she can go on looking after him continuously during the childhood years so crucial to the structuring of the psyche (Exodus 2: 7–9; L. Philippson 1858: 301f.).
8 Exodus 2: 2–10; L. Philippson 1858: 299–302.
9 Freud 1974a [1906–13]: 196f.
10 Cf. Jones 1955: 148.

In the midst of this crisis, Freud wrote the essay 'The Moses of Michelangelo', in which he imputes a reinterpretation of the biblical Moses to the artist: Michelangelo, he says, is portraying the colossus at the end of a powerful movement completed or checked – that is, a Moses who, contrary to the biblical account, does not leap up and smash the Tables of the Law at the sight of his people's lapse into primitive idolatry but, restraining his wrath and indignation, stays his hand and preserves them from destruction. Although the Moses essay lacks the compositional flaws that are so striking in the Moses book, it too has an obsessive, repetitive and circular character. The theme of something in peril, of equilibrium threatened, is common to both texts. In the Moses essay, it is still based on a feature of Michelangelo's work, namely the position of the Tables of the Law: 'They are stood on their heads and practically balanced on one corner.'[11] In the Moses book, however, the author relates it to his own work, which is likened to 'a bronze statue with feet of clay',[12] 'a dancer balancing on the tip of one toe'.[13] In the Michelangelo essay, Freud repeatedly describes his postulated motion and gives a meticulously detailed account of the apparent evidence for his hypothesis. He sometimes adduces proofs that are in fact nothing of the sort, such as drawings that he personally commissioned, to demonstrate the particular movement that in his opinion led to the body posture fixed in the marble statue.[14] Aspects of the sculpture which bear out his view are glaringly spotlighted, while contradictory elements are faded down.[15]

In the Michelangelo essay, which, like the Moses book, was published only after much hesitation and indeed at first anonymously, Freud gives the following reason for what was then tantamount to a passionate preoccupation with the sculpture: 'Some rationalistic, or perhaps analytic, turn of mind in me rebels against being moved by a thing without knowing why I am thus affected and what it is that affects me.'[16] I contend that Freud

---

11 Freud 1914b: 227f.
12 Freud 1939a: 17.
13 Ibid.: 58.
14 Freud 1914b: 226ff.
15 As Martin Bergmann (1976: 16) has pointed out, this last point applies even to the horns, which, after all, unmistakably show that Michelangelo intended to depict a later phase in the life of the lawgiver – namely, the time when, with the skin of his face shining (the horn feature is assumed to be a mistranslation of the Hebrew word for rays), he descends from Mount Sinai with the *second* Tables, having smashed the first ones (Exodus 34: 29ff.). However, several of the authors cited by Freud as having previously discussed the sculpture similarly mistook the moment portrayed: 'We have seen how many of those who have felt the influence of this statue have been impelled to interpret it as representing Moses agitated by the spectacle of his people fallen from grace and dancing round an idol' (Freud 1914b: 229).
16 Ibid.: 211.

was now actually grappling not so much with Michelangelo's intentions as with his own identification with Moses, which had even taken hold of his consciousness under the pressure of the conflict with Jung.[17]

At that time, however, there was still space for ironic distancing. On 13 September 1913 Freud sent Sándor Ferenczi a picture postcard of Michelangelo's Moses from Rome. On the back he wrote only the address; on the front, at the statue's feet on the extreme right of the card, we read 'Your Freud' and beneath this, across the full width of the plinth, so that it is not clear to the observer whether the intended subject of the sentence is Moses or Freud: 'returns your greeting & agrees with you entirely about the congress in Munich'.[18] Freud was referring here to the Fourth Psychoanalytic Congress, the last to be attended by Jung, which had been held a few days earlier. In his answering letter, Ferenczi playfully took up the equation of Moses with Freud, claiming to feel 'especially honoured by the Moses greeting'.[19] As he wrote to Freud on 5 August 1913,[20] Ferenczi had incidentally resolved before the congress to take advantage of his contribution in order to 'discuss Jung's false assumption that you *have given up* (and not just expanded) the trauma theory' – so that this element in the later study of Moses seems already to have been debated then. The specific combination of themes that was to be the hallmark of the Moses book actually appears for the first time in 1912/13: *Totem and Taboo* was completed in the early summer of 1913, and Freud, in a letter to Ferenczi dated 9 December 1912, self-analytically linked the fainting fit he had suffered at a crisis meeting with Jung in November 1912 with the traumatic 'significance of cases of death experienced early in life (in my case it was a brother who died, very young, when I was a little more than a year old)'.[21]

Not long after these dramatic external and internal events, while still at the height of the creative powers of his middle years, Freud published his epoch-making paper 'On narcissism: an introduction'.[22] It constitutes a systematized approach to a new dimension, namely, in short, that of psychosis – that is, in the long term, to the theory and therapy of the severe

---

17 Something analogous had clearly already happened in 1901, although without leaving manifest traces in the *œuvre* in the form of a specific work. Ernest Jones tells us (1955: 365) that, on his first visit to Rome, Freud had engaged obsessively with Michelangelo's statue; this had coincided with the time of the break-up of his friendship with Wilhelm Fliess, another experience he probably felt to be especially catastrophic partly because it played upon the old infantile hurt.
18 The front and back of the postcard are reproduced in Figures 2 and 3 respectively.
19 In Freud 1992g [1908–14]: 508.
20 Ibid.: 503.
21 Ibid.: 440.
22 Freud 1914c.

ROMA - Chiesa S. Pietro in Vincoli - Mosè del Michelangelo

*Figure 2* Picture postcard from Sigmund Freud dated 13 September 1913 (front)

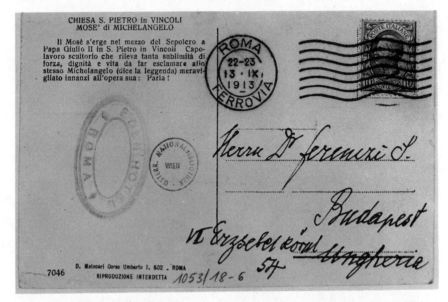

*Figure 3* Picture postcard from Sigmund Freud dated 13 September 1913 (back)

psychic and psychosomatic pathologies *beyond* neurosis. In his contribution on narcissism, Freud introduced the concept of the ego–ideal, and it is surely legitimate to assume that this text, like *The Interpretation of Dreams* at the turn of the century, was attributable in no small measure to his rigorous self-analysis. The Freud–Ferenczi correspondence actually documents the fact that the essay on the Michelangelo statue and the paper on narcissism were so to speak castings from the same mould: in another picture postcard sent by Freud to his friend immediately after the Moses salutation mentioned above, he informed him as follows on 22 September 1913: 'The work on narcissism too is very much in hand.'[23]

When Freud came under the threat of the Nazi terror, he was old and ill. Even more than during the crisis with Jung, he seems to have used the identification with Moses to stabilize his capacity to resist, thus identifying with the prototypal lawgiver at a time of total injustice.[24] From this point of

---

23 Freud 1992g [1908–14]: 509.

24 We should not forget the more mundane reason for Freud's recourse to daydreaming for wish-fulfilment at this juncture, confronted as he was with the absence of a future and with the bodily decay of old age: the Bible portrays Moses before his death at the age of 120 as a vigorous, healthy old man – 'his eye was not dim, nor his natural force abated' (Deuteronomy 34: 7; L. Philippson 1858: 994) – that is to say, as one who remained *independent* to the end.

view, the assertion that Moses was an Egyptian cannot but surprise us. As stated, Freud seems already to have made this assumption about the origins of Moses at an earlier date. Now, however, he felt compelled for the first time to *prove* it, irrelevant though it actually is to the manifest principal aim of the book, which is the development of a theory of the genesis and effect of monotheistic religions – whereas the other hypothesis, that Moses was murdered, is constitutive of Freud's attempt at explanation.[25]

In view of the time of publication – part in 1937 and part in 1939 – it is no wonder that the hypothesis of Moses as an Egyptian, which, as Freud says in a letter to Ernest Jones dated 3 March 1936, amounts to nothing less than 'a denial of the Jewish national myth',[26] unleashed a storm of indignation among the European Jews, who were then about to suffer their greatest catastrophe, and brought down upon Freud's head the charge of distancing himself from his Jewish origins.[27] The hypothesis was in fact not new, but the critics evidently did not know that in the wake of the Enlightenment the Mosaic tradition was commonly traced back to Egyptian origins. Freud could have cited not only Goethe but also, in particular, Schiller.[28] Another point that was overlooked was that, by discussing the involvement of a second, Midianite, Moses, in the history of the impact of monotheism, Freud deprived the 'Egyptian' hypothesis of some of its force.

Reading the text from the perspective of a later time,[29] one is more inclined to see it as an attempt to relativize *one* of the causes of the millennia-old phenomenon of anti-Semitism, which rose to the pitch of a collective annihilation psychosis after Hitler's seizure of power. For Freud is in effect telling the reader that it was not God the Father who chose the Jews to be his people, but the man Moses, who was not only a human being but also a non-Jew; that there is therefore no reason for the siblings to envy this child of Israel so murderously for his pre-eminent position; that it is also Moses who is to blame for the high ethical demands of monotheism, or in other words drive renunciation and the sense of guilt; and that the *paranoid* split between Jews and non-Jews, which unleashes wave upon wave of persecution, need not therefore be impossible to overcome for all time. Perhaps Freud, in a kind of secularized messianism, even pictured to himself in his daydream the possibility that his own

---

25 Freud 1939a: 101.
26 Freud 1993e [1908–39]: 751.
27 Cf. Gay 1988: 645ff.
28 On the reconstruction of the history of this hypothesis and its eventual refutation, cf. R. Smend 1995.
29 For an example dating back to the 1950s, cf. D. Bakan 1958: 327ff.

Enlightenment-inspired theory of civilization might help to promote this collective healing process. From today's vantage point in particular, that can only be a matter for speculation.

One *subjective* function of the Egyptian hypothesis for Freud might have been to establish a distance between himself and the overwhelming power of his identification; to thrust away from himself the figure of Moses, who wanted, so to speak, to take 'concrete' possession of him – by the separative logic of the conditional clause 'If Moses was an Egyptian ...', then I am *not* Moses. There is indeed some evidence that Freud was at times in danger of losing the metaphorical space between himself and this representation of his ego-ideal. The sheer quantitative level of the traumatic flood of stimuli in the experience of being impotently at the mercy of political persecution, serious illness and old age may have triggered in Freud, who, as stated earlier, found it hard to tolerate dependence of any kind, a regressive process that briefly affected even his ego functions.

At any rate, the compulsive, driven element in Freud's preoccupation with the biblical figure at this time is conspicuous not only in the manuscripts but also in letters and conversations. For instance, at his only meeting with Salvador Dalí, in 1938, he is reported to have said with fervour that 'Moses is flesh of sublimation';[30] in 1934 he had already written in a letter: 'The man and what I wanted to make of him pursue me everywhere';[31] and in the study of Moses itself he notes that the work had tormented him 'like an unlaid ghost'[32] after he had determined to put it aside for the time being. In the passage of the book in which Freud discusses the pathological aftereffects of trauma in the individual psyche, he writes:

> All these phenomena, the symptoms as well as the restrictions on the ego and the stable character-changes, have a *compulsive* quality: that is to say that they have great psychical intensity and at the same time exhibit a far-reaching independence of the organization of the other mental processes, which are adjusted to the demands of the real external world and obey the laws of logical thinking. [...] They are, one might say, a State within a State, an inaccessible party, with which co-operation is

---

30 Dalí 1942: 398.

31 Freud 1968a [1927–39]: 98.

32 Freud 1939a: 103. This metaphor also occurs repeatedly in the letters. For example, even in the midst of the chaos and uncertainty of his final preparations for emigration, Freud wrote to Ernest Jones on 28 April 1938 that he found 'an hour daily to continue working on Moses, who plagues me like a "ghost not laid"' (cf. Freud 1993e [1908–39]: 763).

impossible, but which may succeed in overcoming what is known as the normal party and forcing it into its service.[33]

A page or so later, he continues:

> This [...] illness may also be looked upon as an attempt at cure – as an effort once more to reconcile with the rest those portions of the ego that have been split off by the influence of the trauma and to unite them into a powerful whole *vis-à-vis* the external world. An attempt of this kind seldom succeeds, however, unless the work of analysis comes to its help, and even then not always.[34]

This attempt at cure is characterized in the draft manuscript of this passage as being 'usually impossible to bring to a conclusion'.[35]

Can we detect tokens of this quality of being split off, divided into two, in the second prefatory note, composed in London, in which Freud complains that in his Moses book he lacks 'the consciousness of unity and of belonging together which should exist between an author and his work'?[36] Seen in this light, the study of Moses would appear as an attempt at self-cure that does ultimately succeed, as a document of a new, desperate reviviscence of Freud's self-analysis; the peculiarities of form and content would then be in the nature of scar tissue. Perhaps Freud's self-analysis should take just as much credit for his late discoveries about the mechanisms of archaic defence – in particular, splitting – as for his insights, during the phase of the genesis of psychoanalysis, into the laws of dream formation.

Evidence for this thesis is afforded not least by the letter to Romain Rolland, written in the period of Freud's daydreaming about Moses, in which he examines a disturbance of memory on the Acropolis. The text documents on the manifest level the intensification of Freud's self-analysis and discusses 'remarkable phenomena which are still little understood' – namely, 'split personality' and 'derealizations and depersonalizations'.[37] Without throwing their clear, sober argument off balance at any point, the insights gained in that presumed dramatic process surely find a latent echo also in 'Analysis terminable and interminable',[38] published a year later – for instance where Freud reflects on the reasons for the 'variability' of the

---

33 Freud 1939a: 76.
34 Ibid.: 77f.
35 Manuscript page 5.
36 Freud 1939a: 58.
37 Freud 1936a: 244f.
38 Freud 1937c: 226ff.

therapeutic result; assesses the importance of additional traumas, 'the irresistible power of the quantitative factor' in the causation of fresh illness; describes the alterations of the ego acquired in the defensive battles of infancy, as well as the ego of the person who is 'normal on the average', but which 'approximates to that of the psychotic in some part or other and to a greater or lesser extent'; or in the passage on the limitations of the training analysis where he uses the term 'analysis of himself'. Finally, too, we may suspect the presence of autobiographical, self-analytic reminiscences in the paper 'Constructions in analysis',[39] published a little later – for example, in the construction of the circumstances of an early alienation from the mother[40] and in the remarks on excessively clear memories in phantasy-like states – hallucinations (in cases that are 'not psychotic') in which some frighteningly traumatic actual experience from infancy returns.[41]

Be that as it may, some of what Freud has to say in the third essay of the Moses book about the pathogenic weight of traumatic pregenital impressions is surely based on autobiographical material gleaned from his self-analysis – namely, the idea that 'the strongest compulsive influence'[42] arises from such experiences, which are unconscious and incapable of being remembered, if they are reactivated in the subject's later life. Freud may by then have known that the mental wounds sustained through his own experiences of loss while at the developmental stage of profound infantile dependence had made their presence felt in him in adulthood at times of acute anguish – already during the crisis with Jung, but particularly under the Nazi threat – and had on both occasions compelled his obsessive preoccupation with the figure of Moses,[43] the representation of his ego-ideal that was precisely then so highly cathected because it was supposed to guarantee immunity from dependence.

That at any rate is suggested by the odd, otherwise not readily comprehensible formulation at the end of the letter to Lou Andreas-Salomé summarizing the study of Moses, quoted in section II, in which Freud stresses that the problem has pursued him 'throughout the whole of my life' and then asks her to 'forgive' him: considered in these terms, the problem would be that of his own early traumatization, while the moving

---

39 Freud 1937d.
40 Ibid.: 261.
41 Ibid.: 265ff.
42 Freud 1939a: 126.
43 As it happens, Freud does not refer to his Moses essay in the book on Moses, although nothing could have been more relevant in the passage about the smashing of the Tables of the Law (ibid.: 48). Such a reference does, however, feature in the manuscript of the 'historical novel', where it appears in a note (cf. Appendix, pp. 94ff.).

plea for forgiveness would have to do with his own temporary incapacity to control fully the compulsive movement of his thought emanating from it. A passage from the late work *An Outline of Psycho-Analysis* may be also cited here, although it does not contain any manifest autobiographical reference. It stands, somehow isolated, at the beginning of the sixth chapter and only seemingly summarizes the previous chapter's discussion of dreams and their interpretation:

> A dream, then, is a psychosis [...], of short duration, no doubt, harmless, even entrusted with a useful function, introduced with the subject's consent and terminated by an act of his will. None the less it is a psychosis, and we learn from it that even so deep-going an alteration of mental life as this can be undone and can give place to the normal function.[44]

The characterization of the dream as being 'introduced with the subject's consent and terminated by an act of his will' is not applicable to the dreams of sleep but is more relevant to the daydream; best of all it suits the playfully free beginning of Freud's extended daydreaming about Moses and its conclusion, which was no longer under the sway of compulsion.

Once the Moses manuscripts have been critically edited and their chronology has been reconstructed in detail, signs of the bitter defensive battle will probably be detectable especially in the sections composed in Freud's last months in Vienna when his life was in immediate peril. After his escape to the safety of exile, the tormentingly obsessive aspect of his thoughts about Moses does indeed seem to have quickly abated, for he notes in a letter to Arnold Zweig written on 28 June 1938, only about three weeks after his arrival in London, that he is here 'enjoying writing the third part [...]'.[45] He had plainly been able to recover the playful factor in his daydreaming that had caused him to commence the 'historical novel' some years earlier.[46]

---

44 Freud 1940a [1938]: 172.
45 Freud 1968a [1927–39]: 163.
46 It was now possible for the experience of Freud's daydreaming about Moses, and the fruits of its self-analytic study, to flow into and enrich the final works; in accordance with his lifelong custom, that was *additional* to the research results gleaned from the work with his analysands, which, after all, had in turn repeatedly stimulated the self-analysis. This can be inferred, for example, from the beginning of the paper 'Splitting of the ego in the process of defence' (Freud 1940e [1938]: 275f.), or from those astoundingly modern-sounding passages in the eighth chapter of *An Outline of Psycho-Analysis* (1940a [1938]: 201ff.) in which the author discusses the 'ego's pathological states', one of whose possible precipitating causes is that 'reality has become intolerably painful'.

V

Let us once again summon up this initial situation. Freud's letters of 1933 contain recurring complaints about rapid ageing, physical pain and disinclination to continue writing. 'Everything around me is gloomy, stifling to the point of choking,' he writes, for example, to Arnold Zweig after Hitler's seizure of power. 'Fury is mounting and gnawing away at the core. If only one could do something liberating!'[1] The only liberating thing that remained for him in his predicament was in fact to turn away from a reality that had become unbearable and, through daydreaming, to enter into the realm of phantasy.

'The opposite of play is not what is serious but what is real.' It is no coincidence that this sentence features in the early paper on that subject, 'Creative writers and day-dreaming'.[2] In now beginning to reflect about the historical novel, Freud had clearly decided to dispense with the constraints of scientific discourse and to give almost as uninhibited rein to the creative writer's kind of phantasying as he had done long before as a schoolboy, when, forced to sit in 'Egyptian darkness' for an hour because he had run out of matches, he had invented a dialogue between two stars, set down in a delightful letter to the friend of his youth, Eduard Silberstein.[3] With the discipline of his middle years, by contrast, Freud had described the mechanism of scientific creativity as the 'succession of daringly playful phantasy and relentlessly realistic criticism'.[4] Now, at the end of his life, in a return to the attitude of his younger days, he wanted for once to let himself indulge freely his speculative and artistic inclinations.

Certain omissions confirm that Freud, at least in the initial phase of his work on the study of Moses, was quite deliberately abandoning the usual conventions of scientific discussion. He does not quote Karl Abraham's 1912 paper on Amenhotep IV and the monotheistic Aten religion, a contribution that he himself had once inspired and facilitated; nor does he mention Theodor Reik's investigations of Judaism from the point of view of the psychology of religion (1919), although he himself had written a foreword to them. Yet both of these texts contain many parallels to themes and arguments to be found in the Moses study. Again, those whom Freud

---

1  Schur 1972: 448.
2  Freud 1908e: 144.
3  Freud 1989a [1871–81, 1910]: 37f. (letter of 16 August 1873). Beneath the humorous surface, incidentally, we may already discern here the rejected, threatening theme of dependence on a cold, demanding object.
4  Cf. Grubrich-Simitis 1987 [1985]: 83.

involved in his reflections on Moses in the years from 1934 to 1938 were not primarily his psychoanalytic colleagues; Ernest Jones, for example, was not told about them until the letter of 3 March 1936 quoted earlier, having enquired about the new project after a remark by Stefan Zweig had made him prick up his ears. Freud felt drawn more towards the creative writers – in particular Arnold Zweig and Thomas Mann.

The most important correspondent at the time was Arnold Zweig, who had emigrated to Palestine, the Promised Land. It was he whom Freud, after reading *Education before Verdun*, consulted about the secrets of the writer's craft. However, his own fictional construction of the figure of Moses proved to be not to his liking; again and again his lifelong practice of 'relentlessly realistic criticism' caught up with him and demanded that he seek evidence and a solid foundation in historical reality. Zweig assisted Freud in his research, made enquiries of scholars specializing in the field, and informed him about contemporary authors who agreed with him on the Egyptian origins of Moses. By then it had finally become clear to Freud that his search for proof was futile; in the introductory passage of the manuscript of the 'historical novel' he bluntly admits that his results have 'only an indeterminate, if any, reality value'.[5] He was then able to turn his mind back to his original intention of liberation: 'It will be a great joy to have you with me in Vienna-Grinzing,' he wrote to Zweig. 'We will forget all misery and criticism and indulge in our phantasies about Moses.'[6] This longed-for visit actually took place in August 1936; and as the two men read aloud and phantasied together in Freud's summer residence and its garden while the terror tightened its grip around them, everything seems to have been as disavowingly cheerful and relaxed as Freud had hoped. Zweig may have facilitated Freud's resumed self-analysis in a manner comparable to Wilhelm Fliess in the olden days. The writer, for his part, felt so inspired by the exchange of ideas that he himself wrote an essay with a contemporary slant on the Ten Commandments – 'Ein Sinai-Rätsel', published only in 1942 – in which Freudian figures of thought can be unmistakably discerned.

The interaction between Freud and Thomas Mann in those years was even more far-reaching. There is no sign of it in the rare letters that passed between them. They influenced each other mainly by reading each other's works. In 1933, the year in which the embittered Freud could not think of writing anything new,[7] Thomas Mann published *The Tales of Jacob*, the first

---

5  Cf. Bori 1979: 8.
6  Freud 1968e [1927–39]: 122.
7  Cf. Schur 1972: 447.

part of his Joseph tetralogy. Admittedly, it was not until his speech on the occasion of Freud's eightieth birthday – that is, in 1936 – that he emphasized that 'that novel so kin to the Freudian world' made 'the light of psychology play upon the myth' and was 'a celebration of the meeting between poetry and analysis'.[8] Freud, however, will have already sensed this kinship when he read the first volume, which clearly whetted his appetite for emulating Thomas Mann. Again, he knew that he, the scientist, lacked the magnificent registers that Mann had at his disposal, and conceded as early as in 1934, after completing the first version and acknowledging the hybrid character of the text: 'I am no good at historical romances. Let us leave them to Thomas Mann.'[9] That is no doubt why he subsequently dropped the 'historical novel' genre attribution.[10]

When Mann, for his part, composed his short story about Moses, 'The Law', published while he was in exile in 1943, it was not only an epilogue to his Joseph novel but also, as his diaries show,[11] a virtuoso variation on Freud's Moses book. In the middle of the text there is a sudden direct address to 'My friends', precisely at the point[12] that deals with the inevitability of abrupt violent resistance to the Egyptian oppressors before the route to freedom can be embarked upon – as if Thomas Mann were making a direct appeal to like-minded people under the Hitler dictatorship to follow suit themselves, and as if wishing *in memoriam* to render superfluous the exhortation that Freud had made to him in a birthday letter in 1935:

[...]: in the name of countless numbers of your contemporaries I wish to express the confidence that you will never do or say anything – an

---

8 Mann 1976 [1936]: 427.
9 Quoted in Jones 1957: 194.
10 Privately, however, he seems to have remained playfully faithful to the fictional aspiration. This is evident from the following handwritten comment that follows the author's dedication in an offprint of the first published version of 'If Moses was an Egyptian ...' (*Imago*, 1937, vol. 23: 4): 'Perhaps also only a figment.' In addition, the formulation 'that what is probable is not necessarily the truth and that the truth is not always probable' has been highlighted in the printed text by a marginal mark on the first page. We do not know for whom the reprint was intended (I came across a copy of the dedication page in the Sigmund Freud Collection at the Library of Congress). It was at any rate not Thomas Mann, whose offprint bears a different dedication (personal communication from Hans Wysling of the Thomas Mann Archive).
11 Thomas Mann read Freud's book on Moses in May 1939, very soon after its publication (Mann 1980 [1937–9]: 406, 410 and 412). He reread it in January 1943 immediately before starting work on his Moses short story and while drafting it (Mann 1982 [1940–3]: 521ff.).
12 Mann 1975 [1943]: 256.

author's words, after all, are deeds – that is cowardly or base, and that even at a time which blurs judgement you will choose the right way and show it to others.[13]

In his dialogue with creative writers, Freud finally derived yet another benefit from his daydreaming. We may assume that the composition of the Moses manuscripts was accompanied by a resumption of his study of the Bible. This repetition of his childhood reading of the Torah – a kind of homecoming to the security of the thoroughly familiar world of language and images he had had long ago from his father – once again lastingly reinforced his Jewish identity. In the process, as Freud tells us in a passage added to the second edition of *An Autobiographical Study*[14] in 1935,[15] he realized for the first time the extent to which the work of his entire life had been influenced by this text.[16] This in no way implies acceptance of the cliché that psychoanalysis is ultimately theology or a substitute for religion. The issue, which falls within the purview of the history of ideas, concerns the degree to which Freud's early reading of the Torah might have helped to sharpen his psychological sensorium, imprinting perceptual pathways and linguistic hollows that later facilitated his discovery and conceptualization of the laws of psychic functioning. This situation is in every way analogous to his early internalization of works of world literature steeped in profound human experience or of the great texts of philosophy and the natural sciences.

We know that, as a child, Freud studied the Bible in the then widely disseminated edition of Ludwig Philippson, which, in addition to the original Hebrew text, contains not only the English woodcuts referred to by so many authors but also, in the editorial tradition of Moses Mendelssohn, a new German translation and an extensive commentary. Ludwig Philippson, a nineteenth-century teacher of religion in Magdeburg, had been a protagonist of Jewish rights in Germany, Talmud scholar, classical philologist, pupil of Hegel and Savigny, admirer of Lessing and candidate for the Frankfurt Parliament of 1848–9.[17] In his

---

13 Freud 1960a [1873–1939]: 422.
14 Freud 1925d.
15 Ibid.: 8.
16 On this point, cf. the plethora of quotations from the Bible to be found in the letters written by the young Freud to Silberstein; we also learn from this document that Freud had then – as at the end of his life when he wrote the Moses manuscripts – already composed 'a biblical study with modern themes' (Freud 1989a [1871–81, 1910]: 26), which, however, has not survived, because this 'masterpiece of a biblical idyll' (ibid.: 27), to the dismay of the seventeen-year-old, was lost in the post on its way to Silberstein.
17 Cf. J. Philippson 1962: 102–9; L. Philippson 1911.

commentaries he encyclopaedically marshals results from many sciences with a view to proving rationalistically the historical truth of the biblical account. His style of argument and interpretation is not altogether dissimilar from the structure of Freud's study of Moses.[18]

In his late reading of the Bible, Freud might indeed have been astonished to find in Philippson's accompanying texts such words and phrases as 'unconscious',[19] 'disavowed and repressed'[20] or 'the two drives' and the 'entire realm of the drives',[21] as well as ideas such as that the 'physical side of man' constitutes his 'principal occupation'[22] or that 'body and mind' form 'a unity' in which the 'most lively interaction'[23] takes place. Connections of many different kinds can in fact be made between the commentary and Freud's concepts and theories.[24] In his rereading, Freud might also have found that not a few facets of his own Moses imago owed more to Philippson's vivid character sketches of the biblical hero than to the sacred text; indeed, it may have been the attitude instilled in him by his childhood reading of Philippson's Bible that prepared him, in his later career as a scientist, to take the individual so seriously at all and to acknowledge the ubiquity of ambivalence in human emotional life.

When he finished the Moses book, Freud also came to the end of his daydreaming. He was able to relinquish the wish for his *œuvre* to be vouchsafed the quality of completion and immortality proper to great

---

18 Philippson's description of the education of the People of Israel to its role as the medium of monotheistic religion resembles a rudimentary developmental psychology of groups; moreover, even anticipatory echoes of Freud's main hypotheses may be discerned in his convoluted explanations (1858: 302, where Philippson discusses the Egyptian root of the name of Moses, and 995, on the murderous intentions of the People of Israel towards the founder of the religion).

19 IFor example, ibid.: I and 536.

20 Ibid.: 1.

21 Ibid.: 12 and 19.

22 Ibid.: 19.

23 Ibid.: 676.

24 Here is just one example. Philippson's exegesis to the effect that 'the stronger sexual development of woman [...] removes higher interests from her field of view' (18) sounds like an embryonic formulation of Freud's idea of a superego deficiency in the female sex. Nor can Philippson's feeling for anything semantic, for puns, memorials and symbols, have failed to impress Freud as a child. Some of Freud's compositional and stylistic figures, such as the 'model of an imaginary walk' [*translator's note*: literally 'phantasy of a walk'] (Freud 1985c [1887–1904]: 365) are also paralleled in Philippson's explanations (e.g. 52, 292, 541 and 846). Even the 'harshness' mentioned earlier turns up in his characterization of the Mosaic Law, which he calls 'a doctrine that harshly confronts everything that has hitherto come to the knowledge of man' (XXVI). On the paramount position of dreams in Philippson's commentary, cf. McGrath 1986: 48f.

works of art and the great religions. Among the unpublished papers in his estate is an undated note that might well stem from the period after his arrival in exile, which reads: 'Science humbles the individual, greatness shrinks before the difficulties of acquiring real knowledge; each individual can conquer only a small area, each must go astray after a certain point, only the succeeding generations can do it properly.'[25] At any rate, in his very last two writings, composed in London and published posthumously – *An Outline of Psycho-Analysis*[26] and 'Some elementary lessons in psycho-analysis'[27] – Freud described for the last time, in a context strictly confined to what could be derived from clinical experience and emphasizing the limitation and provisionality of his knowledge, that 'small area' by which he himself had broadened our knowledge of the human condition; it was in truth a gigantic area.

In a few places glints of the identification with Moses can still be detected in these two texts, which summarize the basic teachings of psychoanalysis briefly and yet more briefly. Are they not comparable to the *two* editions of the decalogue? Philippson too refers to the '*outline* of the divine law'.[28] Furthermore, in his concluding comments on the Book of Deuteronomy, he describes how Moses, putting his internal house in order before his death, sets about 'a final powerful inculcation of the law and commitment of the people'. 'The scattered doctrine and law-giving had [to be] collected in a clear, concise, summary presentation', in 'popular-homiletic' form.[29] This was to be done 'along both dogmatic and historical lines'.[30] Can it be mere chance that, although Freud concedes at the beginning of his 'Elementary lessons' that psychoanalysis has little prospect of becoming 'popular', he nevertheless compares two possible methods – genetic and dogmatic respectively – of presenting a scientific discipline to an uninstructed person? Moreover, he comments as follows on the latter approach:

> [It] begins straight away by stating its conclusions. Its premises make demands upon the audience's attention and belief and very little is adduced in support of them. And there is then a danger that a critical

25 Quoted in Grubrich-Simitis 1988 [1987]: 30.
26 Freud 1940a [1938].
27 Freud 1940b [1938].
28 L. Philippson 1858: 538.
29 Ibid.: 997.
30 Ibid.: 998.

hearer may shake his head and say: 'All this sounds most peculiar: where does the fellow get it from?'[31]

Yet the clarity and measured aplomb of the message of his two last writings bear witness to the fact that Freud before his death, through self-analysis and his rescue from persecution, felt liberated and was moving freely in the metaphorical play space.

Finally, let us return to the question with which I started: why did Freud depart from his usual custom by not keeping only the fair copy of the Moses manuscripts, and why did he publish the text at all given its conspicuously unbalanced structure? The following three answers may be conjectured.

First, the speculative overall construction and in places flawed logic conceal many substantial new insights, which have been hardly touched upon here. One reason why Freud published his book on Moses was that he did not wish to withhold these novelties from the public. Walter Benjamin's appreciative comment about the style of the works written in Freud's old age, that 'the greatest ideas' are often presented 'in passing',[32] proves to be particularly apt in the case of the last book. Since ideas omitted by Freud from the printed version are sketched out in the draft manuscripts, these sheets were preserved in addition to the fair copy.

Second, the study of Moses demonstrates to a greater extent than any of Freud's other works the depth of his Jewish roots. In the preface to the Hebrew edition of *Totem and Taboo*, written in 1930, he had replied as follows to his own rhetorical question as to what was left to him that was Jewish, given that he was so completely alienated from the religion of his fathers: 'A very great deal, and probably its very essence.'[33] However, as he

---

31 Freud 1940b [1938]: 281. As it happens, the manuscript of *An Outline of Psycho-Analysis* also begins on a Philippsonian note; when the text was first printed in *Internationale Zeitschrift für Psychoanalyse und Imago*, the editors declared the introductory sentences to be a 'preface' and omitted them, no doubt inadvertently, from the reprint in vol. 17 of the *Gesammelte Werke*. They read as follows in the manuscript: 'This little book – work – is intended to bring together the tenets of ΨA in [the] briefest – most concise – form and in the most unequivocal terms as it were dogmatically. Catechism [is however] to be rejected because [it] has [the] form of question and answer. [The book's] intention [is] naturally understandably not to compel belief and arouse conviction. The assertions – teachings – of ΨA are based on an incalculable number of observations and experiences, and only someone who has repeated these observations on himself and others is in a position to arrive at a judgement of his own upon it.'
32 Benjamin 1980 [1935]: 953.
33 Freud 1934b [1930]: xv.

had then continued, he could not now express that essence clearly in words; some day, no doubt, it would become accessible to the scientific mind. It was only very late in his life, when, it may be assumed, the extent of the annihilation catastrophe was beginning to dawn on him, that Freud, in the study of Moses, attempted such an enterprise and also wanted to make his attempt a matter of public record. By not destroying the draft manuscripts, he was leaving us the raw material for further research in the future.

Third, although less obviously than *The Interpretation of Dreams, Moses and Monotheism* is, not least, a result of Freud's self-analysis. By publishing the text with all its tokens of overstrain, and not clearing away the quarry of the manuscripts, he may have wished to show indirectly that it was not only during the genesis of the psychoanalytic paradigm that his self-analysis was a *central* aspect of his research activity. In this way he was as it were correcting the now traditional view[34] that he himself had urged upon us by his manifest emphasis on the role of self-analysis in his early discoveries and by the substantially undisguised publication, at that time, of psychic material of his own. In reality, the self-analysis no doubt retained this *preeminent* function throughout Freud's life, although its intensity varied according to the pressure of his suffering. Precisely in his tormented very last years, it seems to have been the vehicle for his late sallies into the dimension of the inner world beyond neurosis. The manuscript and printed text of the Moses study bear witness, too, to the depth of the distress into which the Nazi terror had plunged Freud, and constitute traces which he plainly did not wish to efface. In this way, by the example of his own person, he demonstrated for the last time some of his great fundamental humanizing insights, which admittedly continued to offend and frighten: that the boundaries between mental normality and pathology are fluid; that the human psyche, which is liable to derangement throughout life owing to its complex development, can be injured by the pressure of extreme political events; and that, as he says at one point in the Moses book,[35] we remain 'childish and in need of protection' – even as adults.

---

34 Cf. in particular the classical study by Didier Anzieu (1986 [1959]), which concentrates on the early phase.
35 Freud 1939a: 128.

# APPENDIX
## DESCRIPTION OF THE MOSES MANUSCRIPTS

It will not be possible for a complete critical edition of the Moses manuscripts to be brought out quickly. The following description is intended to give the reader an impression of the formations and stratifications, as well as of some of the fault-lines, to be found in the quarry mentioned at the beginning of this essay.

The manuscripts, which amount to just over 200 pages, are at present in the Manuscript Division of the Library of Congress, Washington, DC (Sigmund Freud Collection). They were transferred to this final depository from London in the mid-1980s after the death of Anna Freud.

The Moses manuscripts can be grouped together in three bundles: the manuscript of the 'historical novel', that of the published version and that of the draft of parts of the third essay.

## Manuscript of the 'historical novel'[1]

Although this book is not the place for a detailed discussion of the differences between the 'historical novel' and the printed version,[2] a cursory characterization is appropriate here. What Freud preserved of the early version is by no means a completely different work from its printed successor that has long been familiar to us; the former's pages in fact contain the fundamental ideas of the printed version – sometimes in rather different order – in which, however, they are developed more fully and, as it were, orchestrated more sumptuously; this applies particularly to the first and second essays and in some respects also to the first part of the third essay. In the transition from the early version to the book as later published, however, we cannot fail to see how the author progressively abandoned the loose, narrative ductus in favour of a more strenuously scientific style of argument, while withdrawing the self-analytic, autobiographical element.

---

1 As I learned only after concluding my lecture, Yosef Hayim Yerushalmi was working on the manuscript of the 'historical novel' at about the same time as myself and has published the first two pages of the introductory passage (Yerushalmi 1989: 392f.), a piece that had been presented in print before by Pier Cesare Bori (Bori 1979: 7f.). In the context of his retranslation of the Moses book for vol. 11 of *Opere di Sigmund Freud*, Bori also offered an Italian translation of the introductory text in 1979. In both publications he supplied the reader with some information on the Moses manuscripts. It is proposed to publish the entire manuscript of the 'historical novel' for the first time in a new paperback edition of the works of Sigmund Freud in German to be brought out by Fischer Taschenbuch Verlag.

2 On this point, cf. the comments in Grubrich-Simitis 1996 [1993]: 199ff.

A *table of contents* of the early version survives. It is written, manifestly not in Freud's hand, on one side of a double sheet and takes the following form:[3]

The Man Moses.
A Historical Novel.

a) Did Moses Live?
b) The Origin of Moses.
c) The New Religion.
d) The Exodus from Egypt.
e) The Chosen People.
f ) The Sign of the Covenant and the Name of God.
Critical Appendix.

II.  The People of Israel.
b) The Great Man.
c) The Advance in Intellectuality.
e) Renunciation of Drives

III. What Is True in Religion.
b) The Tradition.
c) The Return of the Repressed.
d) The Historical Truth.
e) The Historical Development.

The surviving parts of the *manuscript of the 'historical novel'* itself in fact cover only the themes outlined in the first section of the table of contents. The bundle amounts to fifty-one pages in all, of which the text of sections 'a)' to 'f)' comprises twenty-eight pages and that of the critical appendix ten; a separate manuscript of 'Notes' to which it is not easy to assign a place, accompanied by a 'Key to the Notes' and a 'List of the Main Works on which I have drawn', accounts for the remaining thirteen pages.

Not long after starting work on the early version – the first sheet of the manuscript is dated '9.8.1934'[4] – Freud wrote to Arnold Zweig on 30

---

3  In the following extract from the manuscripts, additions by me are shown in square brackets. [*Translator's note*: The translation is laid out as far as possible in accordance with the original.]

4  Cf. Figure 4. All the facsimiles are reproduced here at substantially reduced scale. Freud wrote on large double sheets measuring 40 × 25 centimetres. In the case of the Moses manuscripts, some of the double sheets have been divided into single pages. Some pages are written on both sides and others on the front only. In accordance with his usual custom, Freud wrote the Moses manuscripts with a fountain pen and used wax crayons – in this case blue, red and red-brown – for marking. *Note for the English edition*: In the original German edition of this essay, footnotes were used to draw attention to the many corrections made by Freud in the manuscript, relating to details of the wording. These notes are omitted here because the amendments mostly concern subtleties of the German language that cannot be reproduced in English.

91

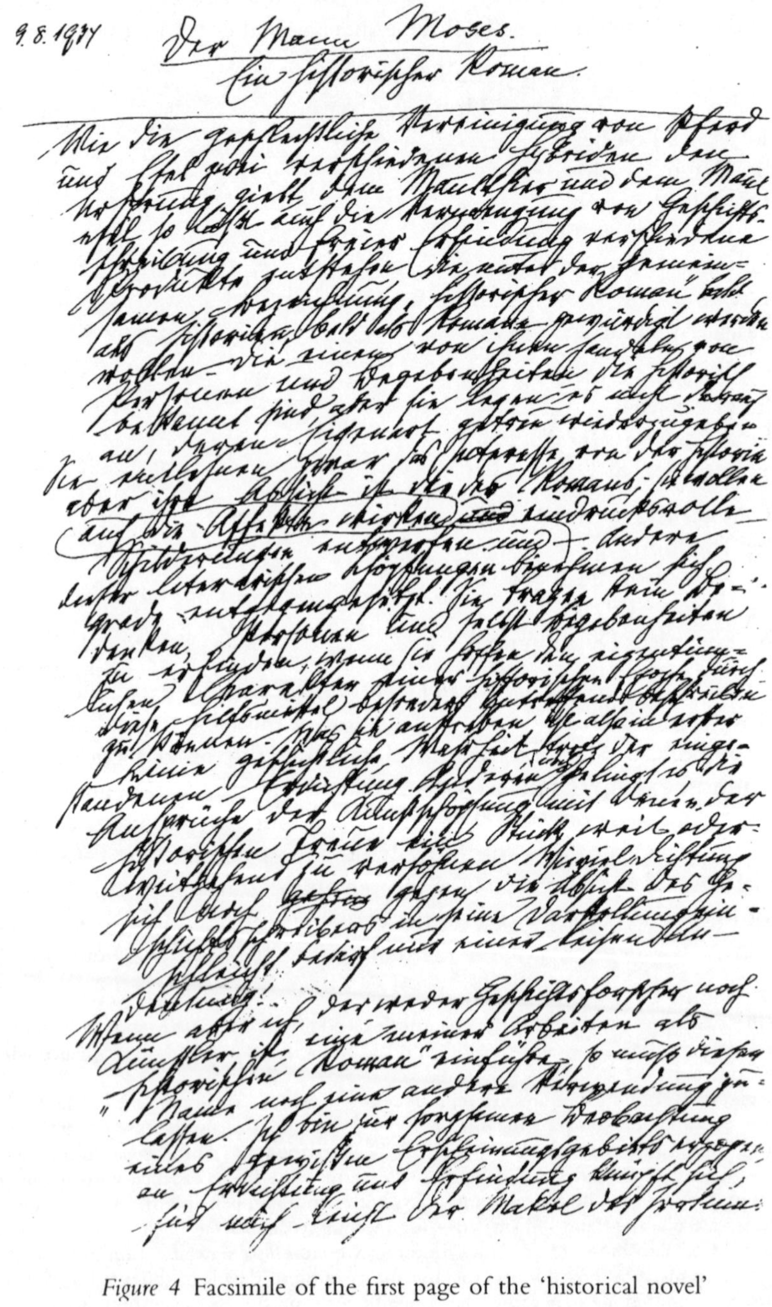

9.8.1934 Der Mann Moses.
Ein historischer Roman.

*Figure 4* Facsimile of the first page of the 'historical novel'

September 1934: 'The material fits into three sections. The first part is like an interesting novel; the second is laborious and lengthy; the third is full of content and makes exacting reading.'[5] A few days later, on 6 November, one of the reasons he gives for not publishing is 'that this historical novel won't stand up to my own criticism [...] and I should not like to endanger the final formula of the whole book, which I regard as valuable, by founding it on a base of clay'.[6] These extracts from the letters, together with the table of contents, indicate that Freud presumably intended to apply the genre attribution 'historical novel' only to the first part of the early version (this would correspond to the first and second essays of the book as published). This means that he did not regard the second and third parts of the early version as belonging to the historical novel, as it were to the 'base of clay'; these two parts correspond, down to the sometimes identical subheads, to the third essay in the printed version, into which they were so to speak subsequently fused.[7] The following passage at the end of the first part of the early version also tends to bear out the thesis that only that first part was deemed to be the 'historical novel': 'At this point I can conclude what I announced as the historical novel about the man Moses.'[8] A similar formulation can be found at the beginning of the ensuing critical appendix: 'I did not know that it would be so difficult to compose a "historical novel". Now it is finished, my conscience enjoins me to apply the criterion of sober historiography to it.'[9] Nevertheless, in a letter from Freud to Max Eitingon dated 27 October 1934[10] informing him that the 'Moses' was 'finished', he writes: 'It bears [...] the subtitle: "A Historical Novel"' – and, furthermore, Freud means the *complete* text, because he continues: 'The structure falls [...] into three parts, 1) The Man Moses, 2) The People of Israel, 3) What Is True in Religion.' However, since, in the table of contents, the first part is not clearly marked with a roman I and lacks a title of its own, there is reason to suppose that Freud actually wanted, in the very first phase of the genesis of the early version, to have the work end with the critical appendix, but shortly afterwards corrected himself and added the second and third parts to his composition.

---

5 Freud 1968a [1927–39]: 91f. [translation modified: 'langwierig' (lengthy) was misread as 'langweilig' (boring)].
6 Ibid.: 97.
7 The fact that the manuscripts of these parts of the early version are now missing may be due to this recasting process.
8 Manuscript page 26.
9 Manuscript page 28a.
10 Partially reproduced in Jones 1957: 194.

This hypothesis seems to be borne out by the fact that the substantial annotations contained in the *'Notes' manuscript* relate to the preserved first part of the 'historical novel'. That certainly applies to the annotation texts marked '1)' to '15)' in the 'Key to the Notes'; only the place of note '16)' seems doubtful. From the notes manuscript, we shall present here in full only the first annotation, because, as stated earlier,[11] Freud alludes in it to his earlier Moses essay on Michelangelo's statue – that is, he gives the reader the cross-reference that he suppressed in the published version of the Moses work of his old age.

In the 'historical novel', the passage of the text to which the Michelangelo note belongs comes at the end of section 'a) Did Moses live?' and reads:

> It [the biblical account] portrays the man Moses as irascible and hot-tempered and itself attributes important vicissitudes of his life to these traits. On the other hand it tells us that he was slow of speech, so that he had to call upon Aaron, who is stated to be his brother, to assist in his dealings with others. Now we are prepared for the fact that tradition ascribes certain character traits and vicissitudes to its great men with the intention of glorifying their personalities. Moses himself shares with so many other founders and institutors – such as Sargon of Agade, Romulus, Cyrus and others – the fate of a childhood under threat at birth and of miraculous rescue. However, neither hot temper nor the inhibition of speech are such typical traits; they are quite individual, to be rated not as assets but as defects, and it would be difficult to adduce any explanation for their invention. In such cases one therefore reluctantly bows down before faithfulness to a tradition which on other occasions appears to be highly unreliable and must, furthermore, concede that the two peculiarities of the man Moses do not go together badly. We can sometimes observe how our small children become irritable and succumb to fits of rage as long as they are barred from comfortable recourse to verbal expression, and we can well imagine that this state of affairs may have become rigidly fixed in persons like Moses. x) 1)

Here now is the text of the annotation intended for this passage:

> 1) According to my interpretation of Michelangelo's statue of Moses, the artist, with the insight of a genius, corrected precisely this trait of the great man. He shows him to us full of wrath at the people's idolatry and

---

11 See above, p. 80, n. 43.

forcing himself to calm down out of concern for the Tables of the Law. These would inevitably have been smashed to pieces had he followed his passion, jumped up and stormed off. Here Michelangelo did not shy away from parting with tradition. A late conception, as it happens, was pleased to present the man Moses as the 'meekest of all human beings[']. Such a character would have ill befitted him for his effectual role.

In line with my interpretation of Freud's identification with Moses, it would be perfectly possible to discern some latent self-analytic and autobiographical connotations both in the note and in the passage of the text to which it applies; after all, the presumably traumatic alteration in Freud's infancy occurred at a time when he did not yet have the possibility of 'comfortable recourse to verbal expression'.

## Manuscript of the published version

The manuscript of a detailed table of contents for the entire Moses book published in 1939 has not survived; this is not surprising in the light of the successive stages of the history of its genesis and publication. As stated,[12] the manuscript of the first essay is also missing.

The *manuscript of the second essay*, 'If Moses was an Egyptian ...', as preserved, comprises forty-six pages (including two of annotations that were plainly added later). It is dated '24/5 1937'. Towards the end there is a crossed-out passage which was no doubt originally intended to form the end of the second essay, before Freud replaced it by the last two sentences familiar from the printed version, which read: 'To continue my work on such lines as these would be to find a link with the statements I put forward twenty-five years ago in *Totem and Taboo*. But I no longer feel that I have the strength to do so'.[13] The deleted passage reads instead:

But I know that my strength no longer suffices to perform it.[14] I shall make only a single remark to indicate the intended result of a

---

12 See above, p. 54.
13 Freud 1939a: 53.
14 That is, the 'alluring task' of examining on the basis of the 'special case of Jewish history' what 'the real nature of a tradition resides in, and what its special power rests on, how impossible it is to dispute the personal influence upon world-history of individual great men, what sacrilege one commits against the splendid diversity of human life if one recognizes only those motives which arise from material needs, from what sources some ideas (and particularly religious ones) derive their power to subject both men and peoples to their yoke' (Freud 1939a: 52f.)

continuation of my work. By slaying the great man who imposed the doctrine of the one God upon them, the Jewish people were staging a repetition of that primaeval event to which all religions owe their genesis. They thereby fell under the sway of impulses that compelled them to make service to the idea of monotheism the principal content of their existence. Anyone prepared to recall the statements I put forward twenty-five years ago in 'Totem and Taboo' will readily be able to complete this allusion.[15]

The *manuscript of the third essay* comprises, together with a table of contents and the two prefatory notes, a total of ninety-seven pages.

It may indeed be inferred from this *table of contents*[16] that Freud originally intended the third essay, like the first and second essays, for separate publication:

## Moses, his People and Monotheistic Religion

by

Sigm. Freud

With two prefatory notes

Contents:

|       | Prefatory Note I                  |
|-------|-----------------------------------|
|       | Prefatory Note II                 |
| I     | The Historical Premiss            |
| II    | The Latency Period and Tradition  |
| III   | The Analogy                       |
| IV.   | Application                       |
| V.    | Difficulties                      |

---

15 The Sigmund Freud Collection also includes galleys for the printing of the second essay in the journal *Imago* (vol. 23, 4: 387–419), which Freud read on '21/X 37' and in which he corrected a few typographical errors and made some stylistic improvements. Corrected galleys for *Imago* (vol. 23, 1: 5–13) of the first essay ('Moses an Egyptian'), of which the fair copy is missing, are also preserved.

16 Cf. Figure 5. The title lines, set down in Latin letters and manifestly not written in ink – 'Titel d. III. Abhandlung' ['Title of the IIIrd Essay'], 'Titel des deutschen Buchs' ['Title of the German Book'] and 'Englischer Titel' ['English Title'] – are in blue wax crayon.

Second Part

Summary and Recapitulation

a) The People of Israel
 b) The Great Man
  c) The Advance in Intellectuality
   d) Drive Renunciation
    e) What Is True in Religion
     f) The Return of the Repressed.
      g) Historical Truth
       h) The Historical Development

Following this list of topics and separated from it by a horizontal line, the same sheet includes an outline of the book's contents, as if the idea of including the two essays already published had not occurred to Freud until this later stage:

The Man Moses and Monotheism

Three Essays

by

Sigm. Freud

I       Moses an Egyptian
II      If Moses Was an Egyptian ....
III     Moses, his People and Monotheistic

Religion.

Again set off by a horizontal line, Freud's own English-language formulation of the title is included on the same sheet, as follows:

Moses and Monotheism

by

Sigm. Freud

This wording was decided upon by Freud himself and used for the English

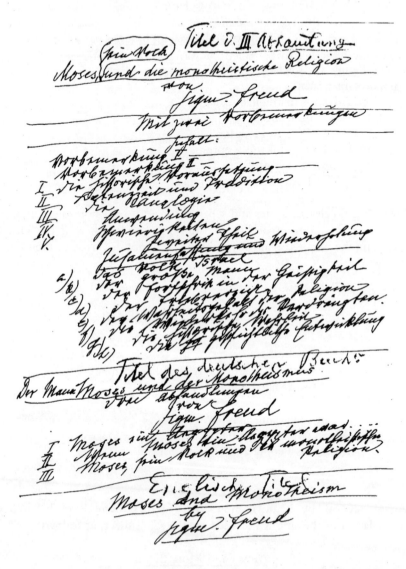

*Figure 5* Facsimile of the table of contents of the third Moses essay and outline of the Moses book

translation of the Moses book published by the Hogarth Press in London in 1939; and although the text had been retranslated, it was retained in volume 23 of the *Standard Edition of the Complete Psychological Works of Sigmund Freud*. To judge from the manuscript, the German edition too was originally intended to be called 'Moses und der Monotheismus' ['Moses and Monotheism'], before the author preceded it with the words 'Der Mann' ['The Man']. Euphony was probably the reason why Freud later also substituted the words 'die monotheistische Religion' ['Monotheistic Religion'] for 'der Monotheismus' ['Monotheism'] in the German title; perhaps he disliked the somewhat leaden alliteration of the nouns and the repetition of the article 'der' in the original formulation.

The *manuscripts of the two prefatory notes* prove to contain a few variants from the printed version. Let us consider two examples from the first prefatory note. On page 1 of the manuscript,[17] the sentence 'In Soviet Russia they have set about improving the living conditions of some hundred millions of people who were held firmly in subjection' is followed by the words: 'They have been bold and wise enough to withdraw the opium of religion from them and give them a reasonable amount of sexual liberty [...].' The wording familiar to us from the printed version, however, is different: 'They have been rash enough to withdraw the "opium" of religion from them and have been wise enough to give them a reasonable amount of sexual liberty [...].'[18] It is as if the militant atheist of *The Future of an Illusion* were flashing once more on to the stage in the manuscript formulation, whereas the sceptical, more profound psychologist of religion of the three Moses essays had gained the upper hand by the time of the printed version, calling as he now does the attempt to abolish religion 'rash' instead of 'bold' and using quotation marks as if to distance himself from the 'opium of the people' metaphor for religion of Marx's 'A Contribution to the Critique of Hegel's Philosophy of Right'. The same tendency is illustrated by the variant of my other example. Whereas the Catholic Church is characterized as follows in the printed version: 'the Church which has hitherto been the relentless foe to freedom of thought and to advances towards the discovery of the truth!',[19] the manuscript puts it much more radically: 'the Church which has hitherto been the relentless foe to freedom of thought and to mastery of this world through advances towards the discovery of the truth!'

From the manuscript of the first prefatory note it may also be inferred

17 Cf. Figure 6.
18 Freud 1939a: 54.
19 Ibid.: 55.

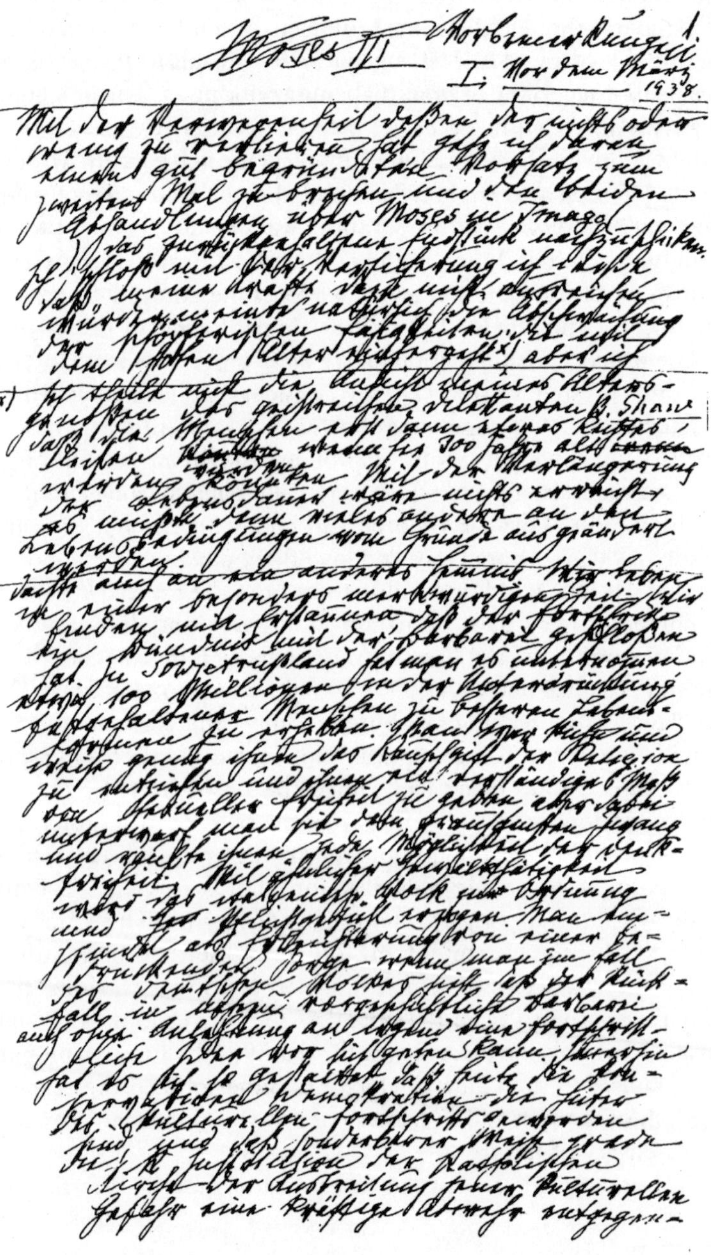

*Figure 6* Facsimile of the first page of 'Prefatory Note I'

100

that Freud may well not at first have intended this piece as a kind of preliminary text, because its end (on page 3) runs on straight into the actual text of the third essay (starting with 'I. The Historical Premiss'), which begins on page 4, the pagination being continuous. The link comprises the short passage reproduced in the printed version in the form of a motto.[20] Subsequently in London, Freud marked the manuscript with the words 'Hier Vorbemerkg II' ['Pref. Note II here'] immediately before this bridging text; he had set down this prefatory note, under the heading 'II Im Juni 1938' ['II June, 1938'], on two unnumbered manuscript pages shortly after arriving in the safety of his exile.[21] At the same time he deleted the original heading 'Moses III' on the first page of the manuscript and wrote next to it 'Vorbemerkungen' ['Prefatory Notes'] and underneath this 'I. Vor dem März 1938' ['I. Before March 1938']. By specifying this date, he no doubt wished to place on record the fact that the text now marked as the first prefatory note had been composed before the *Anschluss* – that is, before Hitler had had himself welcomed to Vienna by cheering crowds and Freud's children had been interrogated by the Gestapo – these events having, after all, taken place in March that year.

Like that of the prefatory notes, the *manuscript of the main text of the third essay* includes some variants. These occur particularly in the passages dealing with traumatic events in prehistory and their aftereffects in later generations – i.e. with Freud's controversial neo-Lamarckian conceptions and the notion of the 'archaic heritage'. The following is one of the few examples where the initial formulation of the fair copy has been hardened in the printed version. Towards the end of the section 'B The Great Man', the latter reads:

> And if, this being so, they killed their great man one day, they were only repeating a misdeed which in ancient times had been committed, as prescribed by law, against the divine King and which, as we know, went back to a still more ancient prototype [that is, the murder of the primal father].[22]

Instead of 'as we know', a more cautious 'perhaps' originally appeared on page 59 of the manuscript, in which, admittedly, it had already been defiantly corrected.

It is also clear from the manuscript that the author must initially have intended to follow the first part of the third essay only with 'Nachträge'

---

20 Ibid.: 59; however, this passage is reproduced in the *Standard Edition* not as a motto but as note 1.
21 Cf. Figure 7 for the first page.
22 Freud 1939a: 110.
23 This is also indicated by the draft manuscript to be discussed below.

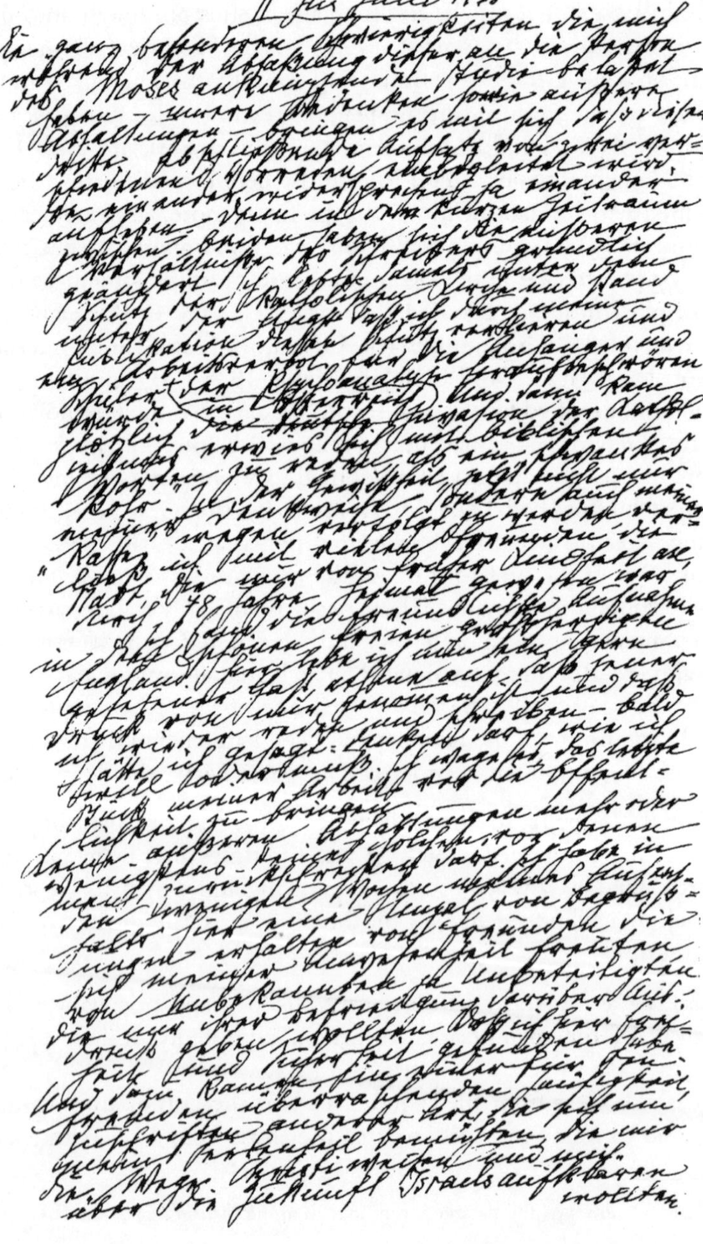
II Im Juni 1938

*Figure* 7 Facsimile of the first page of 'Prefatory Note II'

['Addenda'],[23] but then decided to append to it a 'II. Theil' ['IInd Part'], which he introduced with the 'Summary and Recapitulation', a kind of third prefatory note, composed after his emigration and familiar to us from the printed version.

However, he left out of the printed version one of the most extensive repetitions, still included in the fair copy in section g), no doubt because it in fact coincides almost word for word with the end of the section 'The Latency Period and Tradition' from the first part of the third essay. On the other hand, a later passage in the fair copy, in the section 'Historical Truth', lacks the lines contained in the printed version[24] which explicitly draw the reader's attention to the fact that what follows 'is a slightly modified repetition of the discussions in Part I'. Both the excision and the insertion presumably result from late decisions at the proofing stage, when, in Freud's continuous reading of material set down at different times, its repetitive character must have struck him as particularly irritating.

### Manuscript of the draft of parts of the third essay

As a rule, Freud wrote down his fair copies from drafts. However, very few such draft manuscripts have survived.[25] A particular graphic feature is usually one of their identifying characteristics: it was Freud's custom to cross out the successive sections of each draft with diagonal lines as soon as he had taken account of them in the nascent fair copy. As stated above,[26] such a *draft manuscript of parts of the third essay*, which, except for the concluding passage, shows the characteristic diagonal markings, has been preserved.[27] It contains preliminary stages of the following three sections of the printed version: 'C. The Analogy',[28] 'D. Application'[29] and 'E. Difficulties'.[30] In the draft, however, sections D and E are not yet separated, but are combined under the subhead 'IV Application & Difficulties'.[31] Freud made the final subdivision only in the fair copy.[32]

---

24 Freud 1939a: 130.
25 Cf., for example, Freud 1985a [1915]; see also Grubrich-Simitis 1996 [1993]: 131–43.
26 See pp. 54ff.
27 For the first page of the draft manuscript, cf. Figure 8. The text is written as usual in ink; the 'I.' in the top left-hand corner was put in by Freud in blue wax crayon and the diagonal crossings out in red crayon.
28 Freud 1939a: 72–80.
29 Ibid.: 80–92.
30 Ibid.: 92–102.
31 Manuscript page 7.
32 Manuscript pages 29 and 42.

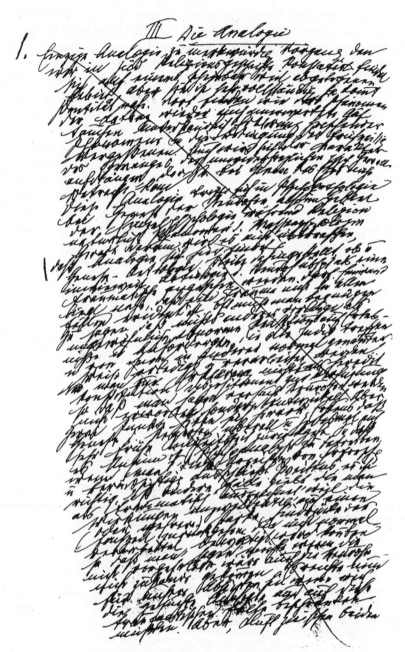

*Figure 8* Facsimile of the first page of the draft of the third Moses essay

The draft manuscript amounts to a total of twenty-four pages and plainly served for the initial terse fixing of ideas in telegraphic form as they quickly thronged in upon Freud, before he elaborated them on pages 20 to 52 of the fair copy. The passages concerned are the ones whose fair copy, as indicated, still contains variants from the printed version and which deal, for instance, with the awkward topic of the 'archaic heritage', the transmission of traumatizations from one generation to the next.

Comparison of the draft manuscript with the fair copy shows that, in the latter, Freud develops his arguments in more detail and as it were at a slower pace, to facilitate step-by-step understanding on the part of the reader. At the same time he tones down certain of the somewhat apodictic formulations of the draft. Furthermore, he added some completely new ideas to the definitive version – as, for example, in the passage in which he describes the detachment of Christianity from Judaism as a process of cultural regression and examines causes of anti-Semitism; or in the section in which metapsychological questions are discussed and a number of theoretical models are superimposed; or, finally, in the paragraphs on possible phylogenetic contributions to linguistic symbolism and the comparison with animal instincts.

The last five pages of the draft manuscript are filled with addenda,[33] only a few points from which were subsequently elaborated by Freud in the fair copy. Brief mention has already[34] been made of some of the basic concepts noted down in telegraphic form here. It should be added that these highly condensed addendum notes, whole passages of which are not readily understandable, also contain indications concerning the relative signifi-cance of necessity and chance, constitutional and accidental factors, in both phylogenesis and ontogenesis. Even on the subject of traumas, Freud says that 'some [are] unavoidable, [while] others [are] like external fates of the person'. From this starting point, he continues his reflections on 'primal phantasies of mankind', on the 'person of the primal father', 'the idea of the great man' and the imago of the 'heroic son'. For example: 'The great man with whom the foundation of religion is associated must be attributed to chance. Impossible to say when he appears, but the events wait for his appearance. The great man is probably one with [a] particular inheritance, with an urge to act out[,] to repeat one of the deeds of the primaeval epoch[,] & who thereby awakens [the] memory of this event in others. These deeds are[:] he sets himself up as [the] primal father tyrant or plays

---

33 This is the other indication that Freud initially intended to conclude the first part of the third essay with addenda, before deciding to append an extensive second part to it.
34 See p. 54.

the phantasized role of the heroic son or both. Moses, Moh[ammed] [are] example[s] of [the] former, the Christ constructed by Paul of the latter.' In a variation on his reflections on the theory of civilization, Freud then notes that the amalgamation of ethics and religion 'does not appear to be necessary'. 'Godless people can be highly moral, pious ones capable of any crime.' This, he says, is a matter of 'daily experience'. The amalgamation actually came about for historical reasons. 'Morality = decision what one may, and in particular may not, do' and has its origins in the will, the despotism, of the primal father. The obligations imposed upon themselves by the brothers, particularly the injunction of 'exogamy & sparing of the totem', are also observed 'as it were in the name of the father, in continuation of his will'; 'adherence to father's rules after his demise was social necessity'. Again: 'What flows from his will is sanctified.' The rational conception of morality lacks 'this factor of sanctity from [the] source of the father's will[,] the mystical background of ethics'.

The above initial sketch, presented without a detailed commentary, gives an impression of the contents of that draft manuscript, which throws some light on, in particular, the creative process in Freud.

# Bibliography

The letters following the years in the Freud entries relate to the *Freud-Bibliographie mit Werkkonkordanz* compiled by Ingeborg Meyer-Palmedo and Gerhard Fichtner (Frankfurt am Main: S. Fischer, 1989) and its as yet unpublished continuation.

'*SE*' in the Freud entries stands for *The Standard Edition of the Complete Psychological Works of Sigmund Freud* (24 volumes). Vols 1–23 edited by James Strachey in collaboration with Anna Freud, Alix Strachey and Alan Tyson, assisted by Angela Richards; vol. 24 (Indexes and Bibliography) compiled by Angela Richards. London: Hogarth Press and the Institute of Psycho-Analysis 1953–74.

Abraham, K. 1955 [1912]. 'Amenhotep IV. Psycho-analytical contributions towards the understanding of his personality and of the monotheistic cult of Aton'. In *Clinical Papers and Essays on Psycho-Analysis*. London: Hogarth Press.

Ackerknecht, E.H. 1957. 'Josef Breuer über seinen Anteil an der Psychoanalyse'. *Gesnerus* 14, 169–71.

Anzieu, D. 1986 [1959]. *Freud's Self-Analysis*. Trans. P. Graham. London: Hogarth Press.

Argelander, H. 1976. 'Im Sprechstunden-Interview bei Freud: Technische Überlegungen zu Freuds Fall "Katharina ..."'. *Psyche* 30, 665–702.

Azam, C.M.E.E. 1876a. 'Amnésie périodique, ou doublement de la vie'. *La revue scientifique de la France et de l'étranger*, 2$^e$ série, 5$^e$ année, no. 47, 481–9.

—— 1876b. 'Le dédoublement de la personnalité. Suite de l'histoire de Félida X...'. *La revue scientifique de la France et de l'étranger*, 2$^e$ série, 6$^e$ année, no. 12, 265–9.

—— 1877. 'Le dédoublement de la personnalité et l'amnésie périodique. Suite de l'histoire de Félida X... – Relation d'un fait nouveau du même ordre'. *La revue scientifique de la France et de l'étranger*, 2$^e$ série, 7$^e$ année, no. 25, 577–81.

Bakan, D. 1958. 'Moses in the thought of Freud'. *Commentary* 26, 322–31.

Bauer, E. 1986. 'Ein noch nicht publizierter Brief Sigmund Freuds an Fanny Moser über Okkultismus und Mesmerismus'. *Freiburger Universitätsblätter* 25, 93–110.

Benjamin, W. 1980 [1928]. 'Einbahnstrasse'. In *Gesammelte Schriften*, Werkausgabe, vol. 10. T. Rexroth (ed.), 83–148. Frankfurt: Suhrkamp.

—— 1980 [1935]. Unpublished letter to Gretel Adorno dated 9 October 1935. Extract reproduced in *Gesammelte Schriften*, Werkausgabe, vol. 6. R. Tiedemann and H. Schweppenhäuser (eds), 952–3. Frankfurt: Suhrkamp.

Bergmann, M.S. 1976. 'Moses and the evolution of Freud's Jewish identity'. *The Israel Annals of Psychiatry* 14, 3–26.

Bernheim, H. 1887. *De la suggestion et de ses applications à la thérapeutique*. Paris (2nd edition).

—— 1891. *Hypnotisme, suggestion et psychothérapie, études nouvelles*. Paris.

Blum, H.P. 1991. 'Freud and the figure of Moses: the Moses of Freud'. *Journal of the American Psychoanalytic Association* 39, 513–35.

Bori, P.C. 1979. 'Una pagina inedita di Freud. La premessa al romanzo storico su Mosè'. *Rivista di storia contemporanea* 8, 1–17.

Breuer, J. and Freud, S. 1893: see Freud, S. 1893a.

—— 1895: see Freud, S. 1895d.

Charcot, J.-M. 1888. *Leçons du mardi à la Salpêtrière, 1887–8*. Paris.

—— 1890. *Leçons sur les maladies du système nerveux, faites à la Salpêtrière, III*. In *Œuvres complètes*. Paris: Lecrosnier et Babé.

Dalí, S. 1942. *The Secret Life of Salvador Dalí*. Trans. H.M. Chevalier. New York: Dial Press.

Ellenberger, H.F. 1970. *The Discovery of the Unconscious*. New York: Basic Books.

—— 1972. 'The story of "Anna O.": a critical review with new data'. *Journal of the History of the Behavioral Sciences* 8, 267–79.

Ellis, H.H. 1898. 'Hysteria in relation to the sexual emotions'. *The Alienist and Neurologist* 19, 599–615.

Freud, A., Bibring, E., Hoffer, W., Kris, E. and Isakower, O. 1941. 'Vorwort der Herausgeber'. In Freud, S., *Gesammelte Werke (GW)*, vol. 17: vii–ix.

Freud, E., Freud, L. and Grubrich-Simitis, I. 1978 [1976]. *Sigmund Freud. His Life in Pictures and Words*. New York: Harcourt Brace Jovanovich; published as a Norton Paperback 1985.

Freud, S. 1953 [1891b]. *On Aphasia: A Critical Study*. E. Stengel (ed.). London: Imago.

—— 1893a (with Breuer, J.). 'On the psychical mechanism of hysterical phenomena: preliminary communication'. *SE* 2.

—— 1893f. 'Charcot'. *SE* 3.

—— 1895d [1893–95] (with Breuer, J.). *Studies on Hysteria. SE* 2.

—— 1896a. 'Heredity and the aetiology of the neuroses'. *SE* 3.

—— 1896b. 'Further remarks on the neuro-psychoses of defence'. *SE* 3.

—— 1896c. 'The aetiology of hysteria'. *SE* 3.

—— 1899a. 'Screen memories'. *SE* 3.

—— 1900a. *The Interpretation of Dreams. SE* 4–5.

—— 1901b. *The Psychopathology of Everyday Life. SE* 6.

—— 1908e [1907]. 'Creative writers and day-dreaming'. *SE* 9.

—— 1910a [1909]. 'Five lectures on psycho-analysis'. *SE* 11.

—— 1910h. 'A special type of choice of object made by men'. *SE* 11.

—— 1912g. 'A note on the unconscious in psycho-analysis'. *SE* 12.

—— 1912–13a. *Totem and Taboo. SE* 13.

—— 1914b. 'The Moses of Michelangelo'. *SE* 13.

—— 1914c. 'On narcissism: an introduction'. *SE* 14.

—— 1914d. 'On the history of the psycho-analytic movement'. *SE* 14.

—— 1916–17a [1915–17]. *Introductory Lectures on Psycho-Analysis*. *SE* 15–16.

—— 1917a [1916]. 'A difficulty in the path of psycho-analysis'. *SE* 17.

—— 1919g. Preface to Reik's *Probleme der Religionspsychologie*, I. Teil: 'Das Ritual'. *SE* 17.

—— 1923b. *The Ego and the Id*. *SE* 19.

—— 1924f [1923]. 'A short account of psycho-analysis'. *SE* 19.

—— 1925d [1924]. *An Autobiographical Study*. *SE* 20.

—— 1925g. 'Josef Breuer'. *SE* 19.

—— 1926e. *The Question of Lay Analysis*. *SE* 20.

—— 1927c. *The Future of an Illusion*. *SE* 21.

—— 1930a [1929]. *Civilization and its Discontents*. *SE* 21.

—— 1934b [1930]. Preface to the Hebrew translation of *Totem and Taboo*. *SE* 13.

—— 1935b. 'The subtleties of a faulty action'. *SE* 22.

—— 1936a. 'A disturbance of memory on the Acropolis'. *SE* 22.

—— 1937c. 'Analysis terminable and interminable'. *SE* 23.

—— 1937d. 'Constructions in analysis'. *SE* 23.

—— 1939a [1934–38]. *Moses and Monotheism*. *SE* 23.

—— 1940a [1938]. *An Outline of Psycho-Analysis*. *SE* 23.

—— 1940b [1938]. 'Some elementary lessons in psycho-analysis'. *SE* 23.

—— 1940e [1938]. 'Splitting of the ego in the process of defence'. *SE* 23.

—— 1945–46a [1938]. Briefe an Yisrael Doryon. *Gesammelte Werke*, Nachtragsband [supplementary volume]; English translation of the letters of 7 October and 28 November 1938 in: *Freudiana. From the Collections of the Jewish National and University Library*. Jerusalem 1973, XII and XIV.

—— 1950c [1895]. 'Project for a scientific psychology'. *SE* 1.

—— 1960a [1873–1939]. *Letters of Sigmund Freud 1873–1939*. Ernst L. Freud (ed.). Trans. T. and J. Stern. London: Hogarth Press 1961. [A second, enlarged edition in German was published by S. Fischer, Frankfurt, in 1968.]

—— 1963a [1909–39]. *Psycho-Analysis and Faith. The Letters of Sigmund Freud and Oskar Pfister*. H. Meng and E.L. Freud (eds). Trans. E. Mosbacher. London: Hogarth Press and Institute of Psycho-Analysis.

—— 1966a [1912–36]. *Sigmund Freud and Lou Andreas-Salomé: Letters*. E. Pfeiffer (ed.). Trans. W. and E. Robson-Scott. London: Hogarth Press and Institute of Psycho-Analysis 1972.

—— 1968a [1927–39]. *The Letters of Sigmund Freud and Arnold Zweig*. E. L. Freud (ed.). Trans. W. and E. Robson-Scott. New York: New York University Press 1970.

—— 1974a [1906–13]. *The Freud/Jung Letters: The Correspondence between Sigmund Freud and C.G. Jung*. W. McGuire (ed.). Trans. R. Manheim and R.F.C. Hull. Princeton, NJ: Princeton University Press 1974.

—— 1985a [1915]. *A Phylogenetic Fantasy: Overview of the Transference Neuroses*, ed. and with an essay by I. Grubrich-Simitis. Trans. A. Hoffer and P.T. Hoffer. Cambridge, MA, and London: Harvard University Press 1987.

—— 1985c [1887–1904]. *The Complete Letters of Sigmund Freud to Wilhelm Fliess 1887–1904*. Trans. and ed. J.M. Masson. Cambridge, MA, and London: Harvard University Press.

—— 1989a [1871–81, 1910]. *The Letters of Sigmund Freud to Eduard Silberstein 1871–1881*. W. Boehlich (ed.). Trans. A.J. Pomerans. Cambridge, MA, and London: Harvard University Press 1990.

—— 1992a [1908–38]. *Sigmund Freud/Ludwig Binswanger, Briefwechsel 1908–1938*. G. Fichtner (ed.). Frankfurt: S. Fischer.

—— 1992g [1908–14]. *The Correspondence of Sigmund Freud and Sándor Ferenczi*, vol. I, 1908–1914. Brabant, E., Falzeder, E. and Giamperi-Deutsch, P. (eds). Trans. P.T. Hoffer. Cambridge, MA, and London: Harvard University Press 1993.

—— 1993e [1908–39]. *The Complete Correspondence of Sigmund Freud and Ernest Jones, 1908–1939*. R.A. Paskauskas (ed.). Introduction by R. Steiner. Cambridge, MA, and London: Harvard University Press.

Gauld, A. 1992. *A History of Hypnotism*. Cambridge: Cambridge University Press.

Gay, P. 1988. *Freud: A Life for Our Time*. New York and London: W.W. Norton.

—— 1993. 'Freud verstehen. Zu einem Essay von Ilse Grubrich-Simitis'. *Psyche* 47, 973–83.

Gilles de la Tourette, G. 1891. *Traité clinique et thérapeutique de l'hystérie d'après l'enseignement de la Salpêtrière*, vol. 1. Paris: E. Plon, Nourrit et Cie.

Grubrich-Simitis, I. 1981 [1979]. 'Extreme traumatization as cumulative trauma'. *The Psychoanalytic Study of the Child* 36, 415–50.

—— 1987 [1985]. 'Metapsychology and metabiology'. In Freud, S. (1985a), 73–107.

—— 1988 [1987]. 'Trauma or drive - drive and trauma: a reading of Sigmund Freud's phylogenetic fantasy of 1915'. *The Psychoanalytic Study of the Child* 43, 3–32.

—— 1990. 'Freuds Moses-Studie als Tagtraum. Manuskript, Text, Deutung'. *Psyche* 44, 479–515.

—— 1995. '"No greater, richer, more mysterious subject [. . .] than the life of the mind": an early exchange of letters between Freud and Einstein'. *International Journal of Psycho-Analysis* 76, 115–22.

—— 1996 [1993]. *Back to Freud's Texts: Making Silent Documents Speak*. Trans. P. Slotkin. New Haven and London: Yale University Press.

Hardin, H.T. 1987. 'On the vicissitudes of Freud's early mothering. I. Early environment and loss'. *Psychoanalytic Quarterly* 56, 628–44.

—— 1988. 'On the vicissitudes of Freud's early mothering. II. Alienation from his biological mother'. *Psychoanalytic Quarterly* 57, 72–86. 'III. Freiberg, screen memories, and loss'. Ibid., 209–23.

Hirschmüller, A. 1986. 'Briefe Josef Breuers an Wilhelm Fliess 1894–1898'. *Jahrbuch der Psychoanalyse* 18, 239–61.

—— 1989 [1978]. *The Life and Work of Josef Breuer. Physiology and Psychoanalysis*. New York and London: New York University Press.

—— 1994. 'The genesis of the *Preliminary Communication* of Breuer and Freud'. In *100 Years of Psychoanalysis*. Haynal, A. and Falzeder, E. (eds), 17–30 (special issue of *Cahiers Psychiatriques Genevois*), obtainable from H. Karnac (Books), London.

Janet, P. n.d. [1894?]. *Etat mental des hystériques, les stigmates mentaux*. Paris: Rueff.

Jones, E. 1953. *The Life and Work of Sigmund Freud*, vol. 1. New York: Basic Books.

—— 1955. *The Life and Work of Sigmund Freud*, vol. 2. New York: Basic Books.

—— 1957. *The Life and Work of Sigmund Freud*, vol. 3. New York: Basic Books.

Khan, M.R. 1974 [1963]. 'The concept of cumulative trauma'. In *The Privacy of the Self*. London: Hogarth Press, 42–58.

Kiell, N. 1988. *Freud Without Hindsight. Reviews of His Work (1893–1939).* Madison, CT: International Universities Press.

Klein, D.B. 1985. *Jewish Origins of the Psychoanalytic Movement.* Chicago and London: University of Chicago Press.

Laplanche, J. 1974. Panel on 'Hysteria Today'. *International Journal of Psycho-Analysis* 55, 459–69.

Mann, T. 1975 [1943]. 'The Tables of the Law'. In *'Mario and the Magician' and Other Stories.* Trans. H.T. Lowe-Porter. Harmondsworth: Penguin, 236–98.

—— 1976 [1936]. 'Freud and the future'. In *Essays of Three Decades.* New York: Alfred A. Knopf.

—— 1980 [1937–9]. *Tagebücher 1937–1939.* P. de Mendelssohn (ed.). Frankfurt: S. Fischer.

—— 1982 [1940–3]. *Tagebücher 1940–1943.* P. de Mendelssohn (ed.). Frankfurt: S. Fischer.

McGrath, W.J. 1986. *Freud's Discovery of Psychoanalysis. The Politics of Hysteria.* Ithaca and London: Cornell University Press.

Mentzos, S. 1991. 'Einleitung' zu J. Breuer und S. Freud, *Studien über Hysterie.* Frankfurt: Fischer Taschenbuch Verlag.

Micale, M.S. 1989. 'Hysteria and its historiography: a review of past and present writings'. *History of Science* 27, 223–61, 319–51.

Nunberg, H. and Federn, E. (eds) 1967. *Minutes of the Vienna Psychoanalytic Society,* vol. 2. New York: International Universities Press.

Oliner, M.M. 1982. 'Hysterical features among children of survivors'. In *Generations of the Holocaust.* Bergmann, M.S. and Jucovy, M. (eds). New York: Basic Books.

Philippson, J. 1962. 'The Philippsons, a German-Jewish family'. Publications of the Leo Baeck Institute, Year Book 7, 95–118.

Philippson, L. (ed.) 1858. *Die Israelitische Bibel,* second edition. Leipzig: Baumgärtner's Buchhandlung.

—— 1911. *Gesammelte Abhandlungen,* 2 vols. Leipzig: Gustav Fock.

Reik, T. 1919. *Probleme der Religionspsychologie. I. Teil: Das Ritual.* Internationale Psychoanalytische Bibliothek, vol. 5, Leipzig and Vienna: Internationaler Psychoanalytischer Verlag; second, enlarged edition: *Das Ritual. Psychoanalytische Studien,* Leipzig, Vienna and Zurich: Internationaler Psychoanalytischer Verlag 1928.

Rice, E. 1990. *Freud and Moses: The Long Journey Home.* New York: State University of New York Press.

Robert, M. 1976 [1974]. *From Oedipus to Moses: Freud's Jewish Identity.* Trans. R. Manheim. London: Routledge & Kegan Paul.

Sajner, J. 1968. 'Sigmund Freuds Beziehungen zu seinem Geburtsort Freiberg (Příbor) und zu Mähren'. *Clio Medica* 3, 167–80.

—— 1981. 'Drei dokumentarische Beiträge zur Sigmund-Freud-Biographik aus Böhmen und Mähren'. *Jahrbuch der Psychoanalyse* 13, 143–52.

—— 1988. 'Die Beziehungen Sigmund Freuds und seiner Familie zu dem mährischen Kurort Rožnau'. *Jahrbuch der Psychoanalyse* 24, 73–96.

Schur, M. 1972. *Freud; Living and Dying.* New York: International Universities Press.

Smend, R. 1995. *Moses als geschichtliche Gestalt.* Theodor Schieder memorial lecture, Munich: Stiftung Historisches Kolleg.

Woolf, V. 1986 [1926]. 'How Should One Read a Book?' In *The Common Reader*, second series, ed. and introduced by A. McNeillie. London: Hogarth Press.

Yerushalmi, Y.H. 1989. 'Freud on the "historical novel": from the manuscript draft (1934) of *Moses and Monotheism'. International Journal of Psycho-Analysis* 70, 375–95.

—— 1991. *Freud's Moses. Judaism Terminable and Interminable.* New Haven and London: Yale University Press.

Zweig, A. 1942. 'Ein Sinai-Rätsel'. *Orient* 3 (1), 5–6; (2), 3–5; (3), 6–9.

# Index of Names

Page numbers in italics refer to footnotes.

# Index of Subjects

Page numbers in italics refer to footnotes.